MW00464045

I HAVE YOUR BACK

I HAVE YOUR BACK

HOW AN AMERICAN SOLDIER BECAME AN INTERNATIONAL HERO

TOM SILEO

ST. MARTIN'S PRESS ⋐ NEW YORK

First published in the United States by St. Martin's Press,
an imprint of St. Martin's Publishing Group

www.stmartins.com

Library of Congress Cataloging-in-Publication Data is available upon request.

ISBN 978-1-250-28611-6 (hardcover)
ISBN 978-1-250-28612-3 (ebook)

Our books may be purchased in bulk for promotional, educational,
or business use. Please contact your local bookseller or the Macmillan
Corporate and Premium Sales Department at 1-800-221-7945, extension 5442,
or by email at MacmillanSpecialMarkets@macmillan.com.

First Edition: 2024

10 9 8 7 6 5 4 3 2 1

For Bob, Linda, Kimberly, Bill, William,
Joseph, Thomas, Kelly, Dave, Ava, Matthew,
and everyone who knew, loved, and served with
Michael. Thank you for showing all of us
how to live like Mike!

CONTENTS

I HAVE YOUR BACK

PREFACE

AMERICAN MAN

This man saved my life."

Those five words were uttered by wounded Polish army second lieutenant Karol Cierpica during a chaotic terrorist attack on Forward Operating Base (FOB) Ghazni in Afghanistan on August 28, 2013. The man the Polish soldier spoke of lay bleeding heavily next to him on a trauma bed inside a military medical-aid station.

It had been only a few minutes since the two men had first met during a ferocious firefight that started with a massive suicide bombing that sent a mushroom cloud into the air and enemy fighters pouring into the coalition base. Yet in that moment—even with both his legs impaled by shrapnel—all the Polish soldier cared about was the person lying next to him.

The man was young and strong but barely breathing. His army fatigues had been frantically torn off by doctors hoping to save his life, which meant the Polish soldier couldn't see his name tag.

Even with raging gunfire and loud explosions continuing to engulf the area around the aid station, the only sound second lieutenant Cierpica could focus on was the silence coming from the man beside him. To his amazement, the man who had saved his life was not a fellow Polish soldier. He was American.

As the soldier would soon find out, his severely wounded American counterpart's name was Michael Ollis, a twenty-four-year-old staff sergeant and squad leader serving with the Second Battalion, Twenty-Second Infantry Regiment, First Brigade Combat Team of the US Army's legendary Tenth Mountain Division. He was from New York City—more than four thousand miles from the Polish capital of Warsaw.

As second lieutenant Karol Cierpica prayed for the life of the injured American hero who lay next to him, Michael's parents, Bob and Linda Ollis, were on vacation with friends in London, England. That didn't stop Bob—a decorated Vietnam War veteran—from saying the same prayer he'd been whispering every day while his son was busy serving three separate combat deployments in the past seven years.

What Bob couldn't have known is at that very moment, his beloved Michael was fighting for his life inside a medical facility on a remote FOB in eastern Afghanistan.

"Please don't hurt him, Lord," the worried father prayed. "Hurt me."

CHAPTER 1

ALL ABOUT MIKE

In 2002, a thirteen-year-old boy sat down at his desk at the Michael J. Petrides School in Staten Island, New York, to complete an assignment titled "All About Me":

> My name is Mike Ollis. I live in Staten Island. I was born on September 16, 1988. I have two sisters and a dog. My dad's name is Bob and my mom's name is Linda. My sisters' names are Kim and Kelly. My dog's name is Sydney.
>
> I like to play soccer, hockey and football. Soccer is my favorite sport. I play soccer for our school; I'm on the varsity team. I am a right midfielder. I also like to listen to music. I like rock and classic rock and sometimes metal.
>
> I am in the US Air Force Junior ROTC. I like it a lot and have a lot of fun in it. I'm on the drill team: we march and do facing movements. We go and do drill competitions, which is a lot of fun. We go to New Jersey and Upstate New York, which is real fun. I'm on the color guard and do memorials for veterans and on national holidays. I carry the weapon in the color guard. I'm also on flag detail; I present the flag and take it down.

My rank is Airman 1st Class. My teacher for ROTC is Master Sergeant Jackson—he is also my sergeant. I have a captain named Captain Kuhn. He will teach me next year.

I want to join the US Army. I want to jump out of airplanes and helicopters. I want to be a sergeant.

Michael Harold Ollis declaring that he wanted to be in the army someday was not a new thing. Since the earliest days of his childhood, young Mikey wanted to be a soldier just like his dad, who had served during the Vietnam War's bloody Tet Offensive. Mike had always idolized his father and even kept a poem about the heroes of Vietnam in his room. The author is unknown, but the poem was called "The Boys Who Fought in 'Nam":

Passed hand to hand, the wishes
The dreams, the hopes of an entire generation
An entire nation sent to war,
A share of old men, leading all our boys to die
While we watched, in horror, in pain
In grief, the disbelief that we had to lose so many
    of our boys
Their FOYs [farewell feasts or gifts] barely left
    behind
Their eyes so young, so full of hope
The fight so long, so sad, the pain so bad
The wounds so deep until at last
Our young men sleep in their maker's arms
Again their names carved in stone,
Never to come home, never to touch our fears
Again, lest we forget, the pain,
The cries, the agonies, the braveries,
The heroes and the smiles, the time
That was so long ago, across so many miles

In a land so bright, so green,
Caught in a place just in between hope and lies,
We must remember still, must promise,
That we always will touch their hearts
While we still can, remember friends . . .
Remember . . . the boys who died, who lived,
     who cried
The boys who fought in 'Nam.

Mike's father, who was severely wounded by shrapnel during Tet, was one of those boys who lived. He had seen the horrors of war up close: from close friends being maimed to some being placed inside body bags in the middle of jungles full of unforgiving heat and unimaginable cruelty and violence.

Bob wouldn't share any of those harrowing details with his only son until he was much older. For now, all Mike needed to know was that his dad was a US Army veteran who had volunteered to serve his country in Vietnam rather than wait to be drafted.

"This picture is of me and my dad," young Mike wrote during an early school project titled "My Dad." "He is special to me because he takes good care of me. He brings me to nice places. He coaches for my soccer team and brings me to his work so I can have a good time and learn about his job, and he takes me to the SportFest.

"Dad, Happy Valentine's Day!" the project concludes. "Love, Michael."

In the springtime of seventh grade, Mike's history teacher, Tim Kielty, assigned a class project about the Civil War. As he later looked for the relevant file on Mike's computer in order to grade the assignment, Mr. Kielty noticed a second file titled "Happy Father's Day." Unbeknownst to his teacher, the Civil War project had inspired Mike to start putting together an elaborate video for his dad that was far ahead of its time for a seventh grader in the year 2000.

Set to fellow native New Yorker Billy Joel's hit 1982 song "Goodnight Saigon," Mike's son had been busy gathering hundreds of photos from his father's Vietnam scrapbooks in order to salute his dad and the men he served with. Mike told his teacher that the special online video project, which was much more difficult to complete using the computer technology of that time, was still in its early stages.

Blown away by what he had already accomplished, Mr. Kielty urged his student to press forward, which Mike did. It wasn't until an eighth-grade field trip to the nation's capital that Mike was finally satisfied with the project, which he had meticulously and exhaustively edited for more than a year. Fittingly, the last photos taken for the video showed Mike visiting the National Vietnam Veterans Memorial for the first time and pointing to the name of one of his father's fallen friends on the famous Vietnam Wall.

"And we would all go down together," Billy Joel, who was always one of Mike's favorite rock stars, sings in the "Goodnight Saigon" chorus. The camaraderie in the song deeply inspired Mike, as he longed to one day feel the same bond that his dad shared with his best army buddies—including those who didn't make it home.

"Dedicated to all the Vietnam Veterans who died for our country," Mike wrote at the end of the more than six-minute video.

After Mr. Kielty shared the montage far and wide with fellow educators to show the power that online videos could have in the classroom, he heard that Apple had used Mike's project in a public presentation to demonstrate the huge potential of technology's impact on education.

Mike expanded on the deep respect he held for his father in one of the last school projects he completed during his high school years.

There are many reasons why my father is special. There are numerous reasons why I admire him. My father has always been there for me when I was growing up. He never let his job stand in the way of his family. He did all the usual father things that are expected of a dad. He taught me to ride a two-wheeler, took me to my first baseball game, played catch, coached me in soccer on a traveling team, drove me to and from school, and taught me how to drive as well.

Yes, those are the typical things that good dads do with their sons. But what I think makes my dad stand out is his love of country and how he passed that down to me. You see, my dad was in the Army when it wasn't the cool thing to do. When other guys his age were dodging the draft or enrolling in college just to get out of service, he pushed up his military duty before even being drafted. He became a soldier and served valiantly for his country. He fought in Vietnam and received the Purple Heart for wounds received. My father thought it was a privilege to serve the country he lives in and now, so do I.

"TAKE COVER!"

Those two words were repeatedly yelled by little Mikey Ollis not on a battlefield but while playing on Burbank Avenue in Staten Island as a young child. While he loved sports—especially soccer—nothing was more fun for Mikey than dressing up in an old National Guard uniform given to him by a long-serving neighbor and playing war. His big sisters, Kimberly and Kelly, would often put battle-inspired makeup on Mikey's face to make his war games seem even more real.

From the moment Mikey first appeared in their hardworking, heavily Irish and Italian neighborhood of New Dorp in 1988, most who encountered the energetic boy running through the street thought they just might be witnessing the birth of a future American soldier.

Whenever Mikey's dad would come home from his job as a mechanic or his mom from her job as a registered nurse, they could fully expect to be "ambushed" by their only son. Other parents and kids on Burbank Avenue had the same experiences, with the most humorous being Mikey occasionally sneaking into their homes or even climbing on top of their garages to surprise them with a barrage of sniper fire from his toy rifle. He would do the same at home with his treehouse by jumping out to "shoot" his two sisters as they got home from school.

His sister Kelly's math tutor, Ed Palone, was so amused by Mikey's ambushes that he bought him a new toy gun. As soon as Mike saw it and said thank you with a huge smile, his face immediately turned serious. For the entirety of Kelly's math session, the tutor watched in amazement as Mikey didn't just play with the toy gun, but did so while shouldering up to corners of the house's walls and popping around quickly to shoot the imaginary enemy. Mikey's focus while shooting from the standing, prone, and crouched positions was so intense that he seemed to forget Kelly and her tutor were even there. Years later, Ed would also tutor Mikey in math.

If Mikey's horseplay wasn't army-themed, it usually involved chasing his sisters or friends down their American flag–lined street while driving one of his huge toy trucks. His dad worked primarily on servicing trucks that delivered the *New York Daily News* to points around the nation's largest city every morning. Mikey loved accompanying his father to work, where Bob would eventually teach Mikey to both drive and repair cars, trucks, jeeps, and even tractor trailers, which helped foster a lifelong fascination with operating large vehicles. It was the kind of special bonding time that could be experienced only between father and son.

There was a significant age gap between Mikey and his two sisters. Kim was thirteen years older, while Kelly had been born a decade before her little brother. That meant both sisters played a huge part in raising Mikey, especially since their mom spent many years working nights while their dad often worked odd hours, too. They did everything from change diapers to help Mikey learn how to walk, talk, read, and write. Even though he would sometimes bang his head against the wall in frustration when he didn't get his way, Kim and Kelly adored their little brother. Later in life, both Ollis sisters would credit the time they spent helping raise Mike for making them better mothers to their own children.

Staten Island's Burbank Avenue in the late 1980s and 1990s was a throwback slice of authentic Americana. From those flags outside nearly every home to kids like Mikey constantly playing in the streets over summers or after school, it was one of those places where all the neighbors looked out for one another and everyone felt safe. Most front doors were unlocked and each kid playing outside knew that their one and only curfew was when the streetlights came on. That meant it was time to hightail it home, wash your hands, and sit down for dinner.

There were no "playdates" and barely any scheduled activities other than team sports back in those days, especially in the summertime. If there weren't kids playing out in the street after Mikey woke up and had his breakfast, he would simply walk over to a friend's house and ring the doorbell or—in some cases—walk into their house like he did when he wanted to stage one of those ambushes.

"Is Keith up?" a five-year-old Mikey said one Saturday morning after opening the front door of the house across the street, which was owned by a New York police officer and his wife.

"I'm not sure, why don't you go see?" Keith's mom said.

Mikey booked it up the stairs and immediately woke up Keith Flannery, who was thirteen years older and about to graduate from high school one year after Mikey's oldest sister. He had been out late with friends the night before and, like most teenagers, had absolutely no problem sleeping in the next day. While Keith's first instinct might have been getting annoyed by the impromptu wake-up call, he adored Mikey and couldn't possibly get mad at him.

After clearing a few cobwebs, Keith was outside playing basketball with Mikey in his driveway. Shooting hoops had become an increasingly frequent ritual since Mikey became old enough to ride his Hot Wheels around the neighborhood. Whenever he heard a basketball bouncing, Mikey would run outside and tear over to Keith's after his mom, dad, or one of his sisters supervised him safely crossing the street. Most of the time, Mikey would bring his toy rifle, which he would position between the handlebars as he headed to Keith's. Upon arrival, he would ambush the much older neighbor, who would fall down and pretend to die.

If you walked down Burbank Avenue on most summer days or evenings after school in the early to mid-1990s, you would find a future NYPD homicide detective and a future US Army infantry soldier playing basketball, baseball, or soccer in the street. Whenever Mikey made a basket, hit a home run, or scored a goal, Keith would yell "FLEX!" so Mikey could imitate Arnold Schwarzenegger or a professional wrestler flexing his muscles. Mikey, who had blond hair as a child before it got much darker later in life, would always do so while sporting a big smile.

"I'm gonna call you Mikey Muscles from now on, okay kid?" Keith said while patting his young neighbor on the head.

On one hot Staten Island summer day, Keith's mom happened to be outside filming her son and Mikey playing baseball with the family's new handheld video camera. As usual, Keith and Mikey would talk trash to each other while taking turns pitching and hitting.

"Okay, that's two strikes," Keith said with his thick New York accent while getting ready to throw a pitch. "Are you nervous? I'm nervous."

Mikey blasted Keith's pitch, nearly hitting a gray Ford Taurus that was parked on Burbank Avenue. He then let out a big laugh.

"That's what you get!" Mikey said.

The friendly jabs ramped up as Mikey, who was wearing a very '90s-style green-striped shirt and matching shorts, continued batting.

"No soup for you!" Keith, who was quoting a now-famous 1995 episode of the hit show *Seinfeld*, said after his much younger opponent swung and missed.

"Oh yeah?" Mikey said before resuming his batting stance.

BOOM! Mikey roped a line drive past Keith on the next pitch, this time narrowly missing a parked Jeep Cherokee.

"See?" Mikey yelled as Keith chased after the ball. "No soup for *you!*"

The two neighbors understandably lost touch due to a large age gap and Keith graduating, going to college and eventually joining the NYPD. Every time they ran into each other in the neighborhood over the years, though, Keith would almost always yell "Hey, Mikey Muscles!" across the same street where they once played ball together. Seeing Keith follow his dad's footsteps to become a cop inspired Mike, who his older neighbor always thought would follow a similar path into the army.

While little Mikey loved to read children's novels like Lemony Snicket's *A Series of Unfortunate Events,* watch *Star Wars* movies, or play video games while drinking a tall glass of orange juice, he was always physically active. There was therefore little doubt he would excel in sports and other outdoor activities. Inspired by Kim and Kelly, both of whom were elite soccer players throughout their teenage years, Mikey started playing the sport at age three.

His ability to speak and learn at the same pace as other kids, however, was a much different story. From a young age, Mikey struggled to meet even some of New York State's most basic early-education standards despite the best efforts of his parents and siblings. It soon became readily apparent that Mikey would have to overcome a learning disability in order to succeed academically.

Frustrated by their local school's lack of available programs, Linda and Kim—a future teacher who would continue to monitor her brother's progress as part of her college studies—went to Petrides to lobby for admission to the highly regarded K–12 public school. The curriculum would include much-needed early-intervention and speech services for students with learning disabilities. To their delight, Mikey was admitted and would begin attending Petrides in second grade.

While school was never easy for young Mikey, Petrides offered the type of one-on-one interactions that would help him eventually make significant progress toward overcoming his learning disability. What made most teachers and tutors want to go the extra mile in helping Mikey was not only his refusal to quit when things got tough, but the respect he showed them and almost every other adult he encountered. "Sir" and "ma'am" were perhaps the most heavily used words in his vocabulary, while he was also known for politely opening doors and pulling out chairs for grown-ups. Mikey Ollis was seen not as a tough guy or wise guy around Staten Island, but as a genuinely good guy.

"I happened to catch Michael in the midst of committing a school infraction. I believe it had to do with a hat or a prank he was playing on someone that ended with my intervention. These kinds of behaviors happen a million times in every school and end with a reprimand," one of his Petrides teachers, Michael Blyth, would later recall. "What I remember about the incident is that Michael was overly apologetic and remorseful. He was genuinely concerned that I may view him in a poor light.

"His reputation was everything," Mr. Blyth continued. "I assured Michael that I would continue to think highly of him and he promised never to let me down again."

Years later, Mike would become a reading tutor for a young

boy down the street named Eric Cundari. Teachers and tutors had come together to help him, so Mike wanted to pay it forward and do the same for other kids. In an essay he would subsequently write in college, Eric shared that "Mike was always patient and encouraging toward me. Whether it was jumping on the trampoline or just laughing at Mike's ridiculous nightmares about Chewbacca, he treated me like his little brother."

High school was when Mike—as he was widely known by then—started to hit his stride. While he had a few longtime childhood friends on Burbank Avenue, they had drifted apart over the years since Mike went to a different school from the other kids. That all changed when Mike took his first small, albeit important, step toward emulating his dad by joining the US Air Force Junior Reserve Officers' Training Corps (JROTC), where he wound up making several lifelong friends.

Mike's mindset while starting high school can perhaps be best summed up by a class journal entry that he wrote at the end of middle school:

> My goals in high school are to be a good student, pass every course, and to get a Regents diploma. I aim to try my best and never give up no matter what difficulties I may face.
>
> Besides academics, my goal in high school is to have fun while learning. I want to enjoy all four years at Petrides. I think I can do this by getting involved in the extracurricular activities. I want to play on a team, like soccer. I would also like to enroll in the ROTC program and join its drill team and color guard.
>
> One of my main goals is to do well in sports and the Air Force ROTC program. I think this will stand out in my school records and will help me with my choice of a college or military career.

> If I meet my high school goals, then I believe it will
> enable me to do well in my life in general.

Something else happened during middle school that would embolden the young New Yorker's love of country and desire to do everything in his power to protect it.

"A serious impact in my life was when terrorists attacked the World Trade Center and the Pentagon," thirteen-year-old Mike wrote as the Twin Towers smoldered just a short Staten Island Ferry trip across the Upper New York Bay. "That was a serious impact in my life because no one knew that it could ever happen, plus it was very scary.

"This is the first time America has been at high alert since the Cold War," Mike continued. "So that impacts me because a lot of people died in the World Trade Center and the Pentagon, and men and women in foreign countries that are fighting terrorism are also dying."

Mike wasn't writing only about the faces of 9/11 victims from New York that he had seen on TV. On Staten Island alone, 274 residents were killed in the al Qaeda terrorist attack. Mike's parents or sisters knew many victims and attended several of their funerals to help comfort and support their families.

Many of Staten Island's dead were police officers or firefighters. Their willingness to make the ultimate sacrifice by running into the burning Twin Towers deeply inspired Mike.

"I see the terror that hurts the city," Mike wrote in his journal. "I hear the screams from the towers."

Emboldened by his hugely successful Vietnam project, Mike once again took to his school computer to draw a stirring digital picture. It showed firefighters raising the American flag in the ruins of Ground Zero—similar to the timeless photograph taken by Thomas Franklin that graced the covers of nearly every newspaper and magazine in the world during the fall of 2001. Mike's digital rendering, however, also showed the firefighters rescuing a young man who looked a lot like him. One has to wonder whether the person being pulled upward by the firefighters symbolized Mike himself being pulled toward defending the American flag.

With his city and hometown reeling in the aftermath of the worst terrorist attack in American history, a teenager from Staten Island set his sights on ensuring that nothing like 9/11 would ever happen again on American soil. Before he could volunteer to join the army like his dad had done more than three decades earlier, though, Mike wanted to support the brave US troops who had brought the fight to al Qaeda terrorists and the Taliban regime in Afghanistan.

"I see our soldiers go and fight for us," Mike wrote in his journal. "I see our soldiers die for us."

Instead of writing his usual class journal a few days later, Mike decided to write a letter that would be delivered to a combat unit serving overseas:

> *Dear Troop,*
> *What's up? You and your men and women are doing a hell*
> *of a job. Keep it up.*
>
> *I just want to say thank you for what you are doing.*
> *I hope you come home safe. I hope you [get] to see your*
> *families. Staten Island supports you and we will welcome*
> *you back when you come home. So be safe, stay cool and*
> *come home.*
>
> > *From,*
> > *Mike Ollis*

CHAPTER 2

HELLO, NEW LIFE .

The biggest research project Mike completed in high school was about Father Vincent Capodanno, a US Navy chaplain who was killed in action during the Vietnam War. Like Mike, Lieutenant Capodanno was a devout Catholic who proudly hailed from Staten Island:

> Father Capodanno ran from his shelter not once, but a few times into the firefight to take care of the men in his battalion. The fighting lasted for hours. He was hit by shrapnel which took off his right fingers and shredded his right arm. He didn't stop taking care of his men. He anointed the dying and wounded with his left hand instead.
>
> He then saw a wounded Marine knocked down by an automatic weapon. He ran over to him and protected him with his own body from the machine gunner. It didn't matter that he was an unarmed minister; the Viet Cong soldier continued to fire his gun, killing Father Capodanno and the Marine.

After sharing some biographical research, Mike turned to the Catholic priest's decision to join the armed forces at the height of the Vietnam War:

> His request to serve in the military was not without precedent. He knew other Maryknoll priests who served, finding it a very rewarding and challenging way of missionary life.
>
> Once he joined the Navy, his resolve was to be a chaplain and go to Vietnam. His enlistment coincided with the greatest US involvement in the war. Just a few days after his arrival, he enthusiastically accepted the opportunity to go to the front lines.
>
> The men Father Capodanno ministered to felt quite comfortable around him and felt free to approach him for good conversation and with their needs. He lived day to day as they did: as a Marine. He was truly one of them.
>
> Father Vincent Capodanno's memory has been honored in several ways. His name has been on eight chapels, several monuments, a building at a naval station in Tennessee, two roads, scholarships, a US destroyer escort, and most notably, the Congressional Medal of Honor.

The grade Mike Ollis received for his Vincent Capodanno research project is unknown. If it wasn't an A+, however, Mike most certainly spent the rest of his days earning extra credit by doing his best to live and serve like Vincent Capodanno and his other hero, Bob Ollis.

Mike's long road to following in the two Vietnam war heroes' footsteps started with his aforementioned decision to join the JROTC. The first two years, however, were not filled with the glamorous marches and drills that Mike had dreamed of since childhood. They largely consisted of pushing pencils inside the Petrides School's small JROTC office.

Even though it was mostly boring office work, Mike still managed to impress his superiors and fellow cadets through his commitment to excellence and something else that had captivated one of his commanding officers, Master Sergeant Peter Jackson. The instructor had seen Mike's Vietnam War video honoring his father and instantly knew the boy who put the time into making it had to be someone special. The way Mike carried himself during those first two years only confirmed the sergeant's initial impression. He might have been short and thin, but he was tough and tenacious when it came to fulfilling even the most mundane JROTC duties.

Another commanding officer, Captain Tim Kuhn, also noticed Mike's hard work and commitment to the program. As soon as they sat down at the start of Mike's junior year, when he would be fully integrated into the JROTC program, Captain Kuhn began to understand how serious his student cadet was about a military future. Mike told him that his dad had fought in Vietnam and that he wanted to follow in his footsteps as an enlisted US Army infantry grunt. He had no interest in ever becoming a military officer.

"Don't sell yourself short or limit your dreams," Kuhn told Mike. "If you keep working hard, you can definitely be a leader someday."

"Thank you, sir," Mike said. "I want to lead in battle."

Mike would later come to understand that officers also fight, but in his teenage mind, the enlisted ranks were where the action was. He never even explored the possibility of entering a service academy or attending college; it just wasn't for him, and pretty much everyone—including his parents—understood why Mike made that decision.

Mike did his best in school and always tried to keep his grades at a respectable level, which usually meant Bs and Cs. Given the learning disability he had to overcome throughout his childhood, that was a remarkable accomplishment in itself. It wasn't that Mike wasn't trying hard enough, but in some subjects, a B was simply the best he could do. As long as he tried his hardest, there was absolutely no shame in earning a B instead of an A.

In high school, there were two things Mike Ollis put above all else: JROTC and hanging out with a group of guys and girls who would become lifelong friends. In the early to mid-2000s, you wouldn't find a tighter-knit group of high school kids in all of Staten Island than Mike and his best buddies Jimmy Carter, Rob Hemsworth, Bolivar Flores, and Quaseem Pipkin. They also had a larger-than-usual contingent of female friends, including two pretty Petrides students named Alanna McGeary (now Saunders) and Kristen Garofalo (now Strine).

"What's going on out there?" was probably the most commonly uttered phrase by Mike's mom during his high school years. It would happen at least a couple nights a week—especially Fridays—when she got home from working a late shift at the hospital.

Linda would then almost always find Mike, Jimmy, Rob, Bolivar, Quaseem, Alanna, Kristen, and other Petrides friends in the family's backyard hot tub. At least one of the kids—usually Mike—would then jump out of the hot tub and run inside their standalone screened-in porch to hide that particular night's case of beer under a table or inside a closet. Illegal drugs were of no interest to Mike, and he was never really able to handle hard liquor. The way Mike liked to party—from high school into his twenties—was kicking back with friends and drinking a few Bud Lights (or Bud Light Platinums from 2012 onward).

The parties would usually end at Mike's favorite burger joint—the local White Castle on Hylan Boulevard in New Dorp. The hamburger chain, which started in the Midwest but later became a late-night staple in New York and New Jersey, was an ideal "drunk food" spot since it was open twenty-four hours a day. Mike would go there so often—buzzed or sober—that his group of friends started referring to White Castle's most famous food as "Mike burgers."

That nickname was only enhanced when Mike—despite protests from the evening's designated driver—opened the car's back door one night and fell to the ground while trying to get his bag of burgers from the drive-thru worker. After lying on the ground for a moment, Mike popped up and said "Well, alrighty then," imitating Jim Carrey in *Ace Ventura: Pet Detective*. Mike's quick-witted response to his drunken mishap had the whole car howling with laughter.

Another humorous incident occurred when Mike went to Mass one Sunday with Alanna. Their good friend Quaseem—who was not Catholic—decided to tag along since they were all meeting up after church to hang out with their usual group of friends. They sat in the back of the church, and while there was some joking around, Mike always made a point to be respectful during Mass and about God in general. He was raised in a religious family and practiced his Roman Catholic faith throughout his life.

When it was time to take communion, Mike and Alanna soon realized that Quaseem was walking up behind them to the altar. Unsure what to do, as they didn't want to embarrass their friend or cause trouble at Mass, they watched in horror as Quaseem put out his hands and received communion from their priest.

"What were you thinking, dude?" Mike said to Quaseem with a laugh once Mass was over. "What did you even do with the wafer?"

"Oh, it's right here," a smiling Quaseem said while taking a big bite as if the holy communion wafer was a Slim Jim from the local 7–Eleven.

"Uggggggghhhhhhhh," Mike and Alanna said in unison.

"Quaseem—come on, man!" Mike yelled while trying to stop himself from laughing. "That's a holy thing!"

Alanna and Kristen always admired how seriously Mike took things like religion, family, and the respectful treatment of everyone—especially women. During one outdoor summer music festival they attended in nearby New Jersey, Alanna and Kristen needed to use the restroom before being disgusted by the condition of the port-a-potties that had been set up for concertgoers. Without hesitation, Mike and Rob cleared out two stalls like they were on a military mission. They then gently placed toilet paper on the seats and floor so their female friends would feel comfortable using the makeshift facilities.

"You may enter, my lady. We will protect you!" Mike said with the accent of an English nobleman while helping Alanna into the port-a-potty while Rob did the same for Kristen. Although they didn't say it out loud, both girls knew that whoever their male friends eventually ended up with would be extremely lucky.

While Mike and his friends loved to have fun—they were high schoolers, after all—JROTC was always when Mike's happy-go-lucky attitude would shift to seriousness. Whereas some fellow JROTC kids would forego weekend activities like color guards and local parades to play sports or hang out with friends, Mike was usually the first (and sometimes only) cadet to volunteer. He also made a point to participate in community service events like working at the local Staten Island soup kitchen.

At one parade in Manhattan that included the JROTC chapter from Petrides, Mike realized that a much younger kid from a local elementary school had gotten lost during the event. After informing his commanding officer, Mike weaved through the crowd on the already busy New York City streets until he brought the child safely back to the parade route. It was the first time Mike had experienced the feeling of helping someone in need—and he liked it.

"That kid is a natural leader," Captain Kuhn said to a fellow officer after witnessing his cadet's good deed.

For Mike, the most meaningful experience of all was dressing up in his air force JROTC uniform to participate in funerals for local veterans. The night before, Mike would stay up late to polish his shoes and every single button on his blues before waking up early the next morning to make sure he was at church on time. With his father being a combat veteran, Mike knew the importance of treating those who served our country with the utmost reverence and respect. He also made a point to thank each member of the fallen veteran's family before marching out of a cemetery with his fellow cadets.

Late during his junior year, Mike found out that the JROTC would be taking a trip to Hawaii when he was a senior. Mike reacted as if his favorite football team—the New York Giants or Jets, depending on when you asked him—had just won the Super Bowl.

"This means we'll get to go to Pearl Harbor!" Mike said over the phone to his best pal Jimmy, who had already graduated from Petrides and started a new job in nearby New Jersey. "You have to come with us!"

Eventually, Mike was able to convince Jimmy to take time off work and join the JROTC trip as a chaperone. Even though they were the best of friends who would constantly hang out and party together, Jimmy's job was to supervise Mike, Rob, and Bolivar while on vacation thousands of miles from home. It was a tall task.

There were also much older adult chaperones, of course, including two Petrides teachers named Lissa and Maryellen. While both knew Mike loved to have fun, they also noticed a maturity that was unusual for someone his age. On bus rides through the beautiful Hawaiian hills and sunsets, Mike would talk about his post-Petrides plans, including joining the army. Unlike most teenagers, he simultaneously seemed to understand the huge impact that choosing a military career would have not just on him, but also on his family and friends.

Nowhere was Mike's maturity more apparent than during a group hike up the steep Diamond Head volcano. As noted on the state of Hawaii's website, the 0.8-mile walk from the parking lot to the crater floor "becomes uneven and steep, requiring caution and appropriate footwear." Lissa and Maryellen were not only both afraid of heights but also anxious about the safety of the kids they were in the Aloha State to chaperone. Thankfully, one of the teenagers in the group stepped up and made sure they knew he had their backs.

"It was Michael who got me through it," Lissa later wrote in a letter to Bob and Linda. "At each level when it got steeper and more difficult, he was behind me, promising me he would be there and helping me forward."

There were plenty of less stressful moments on the trip, as they were on a Hawaiian vacation, after all. The fun started when Mike realized there was a hula-dancing class for pregnant women at a community center near the YWCA camp facility where the JROTC group was staying. Mike, Rob, and Bolivar quickly went into town to buy hula skirts and coconut bras before Jimmy realized what they were up to. As soon as Mike presented Jimmy with his own set of Hawaiian women's clothes, however, Jimmy was causing mischief right beside his buddies.

A few minutes into the class, one of the pregnant women turned around and gasped when she saw four silly, scantily clad teenage boys dancing right along with her. While most women in the class thought the prank was funny, the instructor did not. She chased all four guys back to the campground while Mike and his friends nearly died, not from sprinting in the heat, but from laughing their heads off while doing it.

The next day, Mike once again grew serious when the subject turned to the military. While visiting Schofield Barracks, the home of the US Army's Twenty-Fifth Infantry Division on the island of Oahu, Mike was both fascinated and humbled when a tour guide showed him bullet holes that remain in some of the base's walls from the Japanese attack that thrust the United States into World War II.

"This isn't a scene from some movie, Jimmy," Mike said. "This is the real deal—actual American history."

He was even more affected by visiting Pearl Harbor—especially the USS *Arizona* Memorial, which marks the final place of rest for 1,102 US Navy sailors and US Marines. Just as visiting the Vietnam Veterans Memorial in eighth grade and Ground Zero soon after the terrorist attack on his city had been, seeing Pearl Harbor in person was a transformative experience that reaffirmed why Mike wanted to serve his country. Seeing oil still seep out of the sunken ship and knowing that more than a thousand American heroes were resting under the stirring memorial was a memory that Mike would always carry.

"You guys, that was the best trip we've ever had," Mike said before his JROTC group flew back to New York. "If I was ever going to get a chance to see all this amazing stuff, I'm glad it was with the three of you."

Even though his ultimate goal wasn't getting a high GPA, acing the SATs, and going to college like most of his friends, Mike was still a normal high school kid. He played soccer and went to the prom with a beautiful brunette named Katherine, who was quickly becoming a serious girlfriend. As Chazz Palminteri's gangster character Sonny said in one of Mike's favorite movies, *A Bronx Tale*, "You only get three great women in your lifetime." Katherine appeared to be the first great woman of Mike's young life.

Katherine had made clear to Mike that she was headed to college after graduation, while he had done the same about aspiring to a military career. Like many high school couples, Mike and

Katherine thought their love could overcome even the longest of distances.

On his seventeenth birthday, the plan Mike had been cultivating since dressing up in that old National Guard uniform and running around ambushing people on Burbank Avenue became official. He went to Staten Island's US Army recruiting office while carrying an official letter known as a Memorandum of Record to Military Recruiters from his JROTC instructor, Master Sergeant Jackson:

> I have instructed Cadet Michael Ollis for over three years, and he continues to be an important part of the AFJROTC. Cadet Michael Ollis has achieved the rank of Cadet Captain in the AFJROTC NY-20001 program.
>
> He has been Color Guard Commander, Flight Commander and is currently the Deputy Group Commander of the Corp.
>
> He is a very dedicated and committed cadet since becoming part of the AFJROTC program. I am sure he will continue in his leadership abilities when he enters military service.

With the eventual written permission of his parents, Mike would enlist in the US Army's delayed-entry program. He would ship out to training just before his eighteenth birthday the following September, which meant he'd have one last summer in Staten Island after graduating from Petrides.

Bob initially didn't know that Mike had even gone to the local recruiting office until Mike presented him and Linda with the Parental/Guardian Consent for Enlistment form to sign. Despite some apprehension given his own experience in Vietnam, Bob—as he explained to Linda—knew that refusing to sign the form would only serve to delay Mike's enlistment by a year. Joining the United States Army was his lifelong dream, and even as a veteran who had seen the terrible reality of war up close, Bob would not stand in his son's way. Despite her own concerns as a mother who cared deeply about her only son, Linda agreed.

The recruiter, Bob, Linda, and Mike signed the enlistment paperwork on September 27, 2005. At that time, the US military had been at war for just under four years in Afghanistan and in Iraq for less than three. Despite some serious setbacks in both conflicts, Bob doubted either war would be ongoing by the time Mike waited the required year, completed boot camp and then additional training, and ultimately received his orders. This isn't Vietnam, Bob thought, while giving himself a reassuring nod.

As graduation approached, Mike was excelling in JROTC, having the time of his life with his friends, and falling even more in love with Katherine. The parties in his backyard were becoming more frequent, with Kim and her husband, Bill Loschiavo, sometimes coming to Staten Island from their new house in central New Jersey to join the fun as quasi chaperones. Kim was pregnant at the time with the couple's first son, William, and since she wasn't drinking, took it upon herself to ensure that neither Mike nor any of his friends got behind the wheel of a car after drinking beer.

"Give me your keys right now, young man!" Kim said to Mike during one of that year's many hot tub parties.

"Whatever, you're not my mom!" replied Mike, but not in an angry tone of voice. He instead smiled and laughed before flinging his keys to his big sister. "Love ya, Kim."

At some point during that eventful year of 2006, Mike sat down and summarized his memorable time at Petrides for his final high school yearbook:

> September 1995. This was the first year the Petrides School, also known as PS 80, was open for business. I enrolled in 2nd grade. Not because I wanted to; I really had nothing

to do with it. I was perfectly happy in my neighborhood elementary school. My mother, however, had different ideas. She thought that this new school had something more to offer, like a high school, I guess. Anyway, here I am more than 10 years later. I could have left when I finished 8th grade like a lot of other kids did. But by then, I was used to the place. Besides, my closest friends were staying on, so I did also.

Petrides is different from what I know about other secondary schools. Where else do you bump into kindergarten kids in the hallways when you're supposed to be in high school? All the teachers know you. I mean all of them from grammar school on up. You're suddenly not that sweet kid they think they remember you as. Well anyway, Petrides has been half my life as I know it. So it will be very strange leaving it. I could talk a lot about those first six years but that's not what this yearbook is about. This is all about Petrides, the HIGH SCHOOL years.

Okay, freshman year was new even though the building was the same. New faces came to the school. Some of my friends were older. 9th grade gave me a little more freedom around the school, but there was also more responsibility. I joined the ROTC. I did flag detail every morning. The ROTC was something that I really liked. It kept me out of gym class. It helped me maintain a decent grade point average.

In sophomore year the classes got more interesting. There was no more "Freshmen Fridays" to dread. The girls also got more interesting, although harder to understand. ROTC gave me an opportunity to do a little traveling without my parents. I got to take a trip to Chicago, Illinois, and to Colorado to see the Air Force Academy.

With junior year, the realization came that high school

was nearing an end. I guess the class ring thing did it. I had been playing soccer all along, but now I became captain of the varsity team. It was a privilege. Although it was never a winning team, I did play my heart out. I only got sent to the hospital twice, both times for smashing heads with an opponent. It was the best fun ever.

No one would ever believe that I actually got an award from the Elks Lodge for "teenager of the year." This third year was also kind of sad because some of my closest friends, who were a year older, graduated.

Now it's really the final chapter of the Petrides story. I'm a senior. I really got here. It's not a dream. It's really happening! So far, this year has been the most different and the most fun. First of all, I'm driving to school with my own four wheels. Joy! I'm out of the house more than ever. Great joy! Besides school, I've been working a lot here and there. I do odd jobs. I tutor. I also party hard. I've been chilling out with my friends more than ever since I don't have a heavy school load.

This last year has been the best of all. Although I look forward to graduation, I am a little sorry to see it come to an end. But I know that the best years are still ahead of me.

Goodbye Petrides. Hello new life!

On the last day of school, Mike bid farewell to his friends—even though he knew he'd see them all in his backyard later that night to kick off a summer full of graduation festivities with another huge hot tub party replete with great stories, cold beer, and hearty laughs. Instead of heading home with Katherine, he gave his girlfriend a kiss on the cheek and said he'd meet her in an hour. There was one last thing Mike wanted to do first.

Mike knew he was headed to basic training in a few months, and considering that most of that summer would involve hanging out and drinking, it was important to run laps every single day. He then jogged out to the track, took off his high school backpack for the last time, and sat down for a moment in the stands. Before he took off running, he wanted to take a deep breath and reread a graduation card he'd gotten earlier that day from his commanding JROTC officers:

> *Mike,*
> *Always remember that you <u>must</u> stick things out to the end.*
> *In our business, if we don't, lives are at stake. Constantly*
> *strive to take all the training you can get your hands on*
> *and you will be prepared to meet the enemy and survive.*
> > *God bless,*
> > *Captain Kuhn*

> *Mike,*
> *You'll need to know this; the past is what happens before*
> *you make the right decision. Always learn from your mis-*
> *takes and you'll grow to become a great leader.*
> > *God bless,*
> > *Master Sergeant Jackson*

As the wind whipped through his short brown hair while running around the track, the slender, relatively short, soon-to-be eighteen-year-old US Army recruit kept going until he couldn't physically take another step. Satisfied with his impromptu workout, Mike then looked up to the blue skies above Staten Island, wiped the sweat from his forehead, and said a quick prayer.

"God, please help me be the best soldier I can be," Mike said. "Help me be strong and brave like Father Capodanno, who I know is sitting up there with you right now."

As he picked up his backpack and walked off the track that surrounds the soccer field where he had played countless games since childhood, Mike again looked up, this time toward the American flag. Just as he had when drawing the 9/11 firefighter picture on his computer, Mike felt a pull not only to avenge the terrorist attack on his city but also to defend the defenseless and—perhaps most important—make his father proud.

When he lowered his head and began walking away from his high school track, the future soldier couldn't have known what would someday stand in that very spot: a massive bronze statue of a US Army staff sergeant named Michael Ollis.

CHAPTER 3

HOOAH!

*H*ooah!

"Uttered at award ceremonies, bellowed in formations and repeated before, during and after training missions—no matter how one might spell the word—'hooah' is an expression of high morale, strength and confidence."

This definition appeared at the top of a postcard that newly enlisted US Army Private First Class (PFC) Michael Ollis mailed home to his parents in Staten Island on September 15, 2006—the day before his eighteenth birthday. Mike had arrived for boot camp at Fort Benning, near Georgia's border with Alabama, about six weeks earlier. Unlike several fellow recruits, Mike had entered basic training as a PFC due to his JROTC experience in high school.

"Hey guys, I got you a postcard of the word 'hooah' and the meaning of it," he wrote. "It made me think of the strength you guys give me to make it through the days. Love, Mike."

"P.S. Practice this word with William please!" he added.

Mike was referring to his oldest nephew, who was two and a half years old. He adored William, and no longer getting the chance to hold his nephew and watch him grow up was Mike's earliest glimpse into the stark realities of military life. He also worried about potentially missing William's next birthday party in early January and the birth of his second nephew, who was due sometime in December.

Over the next few years, many milestones celebrated by family and friends would occur without Mike having the opportunity to be there. It was a tough adjustment after growing up inside such tight-knit groups of family and friends.

As he sat on a jet flying from New York to Georgia in early August, Mike wrote two letters. The first was to his girlfriend, Katherine:

> *Hey K,*
> *It's your first letter. I'm on the plane, thinking about you of course and listening to music on my way to Basic. I miss you a lot and I love you. You're a great girl, the best I've ever had.*
>
> *I just want you to take care of yourself and don't be upset because I'll be back. Time flies fast.*
> > *Love,*
> > *Mike*

The second letter the still seventeen-year-old recruit wrote on August 3, 2006, was to his parents:

> *Hey Mom and Dad,*
> *I'm on the plane and have nothing better to do. I just want to say I love you. You guys did a lot for me and I thank you. Sorry for being a pain in the ass, but you guys are the best parents ever. And Mom, I'm sorry that I'm going to be an infantryman. I know it must be tough for you but thank you for supporting me.*
>
> *And Dad, thanks for the talks that we had in the base-*

ment. Those talks helped me out a lot, and I don't want to let you guys down.

Love,
Mike

Mike's letter ended with a postscript asking his parents to mail photos from the party they had thrown at their house before their son left home. Guests included dozens of relatives, friends, and his girlfriend, who was about to head off to college. Katherine wrote Mike a new letter every single day he was at basic training.

"I'm listening to Dave Matthews Band right now . . . I'm skipping over 'Crash Into Me,' I hope that's okay," Katherine wrote. "There are some days, like today, where I really am just still a mess about you, like right now. I'm listening to DMB and I just keep seeing us driving down the Garden State Parkway listening to this same music going to and from Long Beach Island. I'm actually crying—I miss you."

Life had changed so much—and so quickly—after Mike's last full summer in Staten Island. The days of going to Dave Matthews Band concerts and taking trips to the Jersey Shore were over, at least for now. Mike realized that as soon as his hair—which was always short, but never "army short"—was shaved off by a Fort Benning barber before Mike's new drill instructor ordered him to run back to the barracks and clean the head (a common military term for toilets). Party time was truly over.

Mike often thought about one of his best friends from back home, Bolivar, who was also in boot camp. He had enlisted in the Marine Corps, which meant Bolivar was training one state away on South Carolina's legendary Parris Island. Mike knew it would be difficult, if not impossible, to communicate with Bolivar while they were both in basic training. He asked his parents to try to track down Bolivar's new address, but so far they weren't having much luck.

On August 14, 2006, the day before the formal start of boot camp, Mike found out that his big sister, Kim, and her husband, Bill, were expecting their second son:

> Hey Mom and Dad,
> I start training tomorrow. I hope I can call you guys tomorrow. I heard the news about Kim: it's a boy! That's great news. Well, tell Kim she should name the kid Michael, you know, 'cause that's a good name.
> The guys I'm with now are cool. I hope when I get down range I will still be with them. I can't wait to train—I hope I can do it. I love you guys and please write back as soon as possible. There's another letter already sent to the house—it's for Rob. Please call him and let him know.
>
> Love,
> Mike

No matter how many movies or training videos a future military recruit is shown, nothing can ever truly prepare a civilian for the sudden transition to military life. Decisions you've spent your entire life taking for granted—when to make your bed, eat lunch, or even use the restroom—are suddenly made for you by drill instructors who will sometimes get right up in your face and make sure there's no doubt that their orders are understood. For the next ten-plus weeks, "Sir, yes sir!" would be the most common phrase in Mike's vocabulary.

Master Sergeant Peter Jackson, Mike's JROTC instructor, understood exactly what his former student was up against. He wrote to Mike shortly after boot camp formally began:

> PFC Ollis,
> I know you are going through a lot right now; it seems totally different than Petrides School. You're right! This is

*the "real world," no more spoons and no more videos and
yes, no more "sweet" captain to hold your hand.*

*No, I'm not trying to discourage you or cause you
depression; my motives are clear. You are there for a reason;
you chose to be. So get tough and make it happen. You can
do it!*

*At Petrides, there was always "extra credit," "second
chances" and of course a great man named Captain Tim
Kuhn. Now, your commanding officer doesn't even know
your name, Mike Ollis. I say this because I knew you and
who you were the day I saw your father's tribute video. I
said to myself, "this is a special guy."*

*You became group commander when everyone thought
you didn't have what it takes. You proved them wrong, but I
knew you could do it. Hang in there, son!*

> *Take care,*
> *Master Sergeant Jackson*

Master Sergeant Jackson's letters meant the world to Mike. A
few days after the first one, he received another.

"So, another day. You've learned something new or different.
Always remember to train hard because when that day comes,
you'll need it; the training will get you through it," Master Sergeant Jackson wrote. "I'm proud of you! You keep it up and don't
fall behind. Go that extra mile and don't let them defeat you."

Mike would often hear from someone else who had conquered
boot camp many years prior, his dad:

Hey Mike!
*I hope everything is going well. I am glad that you are do-
ing good on the rifle range. Just have patience and don't be
afraid to ask the drill sergeant questions if you aren't sure.
I'm sending some foot powder to keep your feet dry. How*

do your boots fit? That could be the problem with your blisters. Or maybe it's just that they are new.

Please stop worrying about disappointing your mother and me. We are extremely proud of what you are doing now.

Jimmy stopped in to say "hello." He said that he is working long hours on his job. You're right—he's a good friend to you.

Rob was here last night. He was saying that there is no one left to pal around with. He looked very sad. We had a nice talk. He said that he wrote three letters to you but hasn't mailed them yet. He also said he would stop by next week to talk again.

Do you need any phone cards? Let me know. I'm glad that you are working out extra. I have no doubt in my mind that you will pass PT [physical training] and qualify.

Happy early birthday! Can't wait to see you in November. Keep up the good work. Love and miss you.

> *Love,*
> *Pop*

> *P.S. William is doing a lot more talking and I am taking good care of your truck.*

In addition to the blisters on his feet, Mike told his parents that he had come down with pink eye—in both eyes.

"I went on sick call and they gave me stuff to take care of it. Don't worry," Mike wrote. "I didn't miss any training, thank God.

"I'm kind of nervous about qualifying with the M-16. If I don't qualify with it, I don't pass and I can't graduate. It's scary," he continued. "I just want to do something on my own and be good at it. I'm really nervous. I don't want to fail."

Mike went into even greater detail in another letter to his parents dated August 23, 2006:

Dear Mom and Dad,

Yesterday we did our first road march. We marched three miles with our packs on our backs and M-16s in our hands. It was fun, but my feet got a little cut up. We did Land Nav [navigation] as well. It was cool being in the woods but the bugs in Georgia are freakin' scary!

Today was fun too; we got to see two Claymore mines blow up. It was awesome, but the explosion isn't like in the movies. You can feel the impact, though. They gave us fake ones when we learned how to set up the Claymore mines.

Tomorrow we're learning about chemical weapons and Friday we go train in the gas chamber. I'm a little nervous, but anyway, thanks for the letters, pictures and stamps.

How is everyone? Thank you for being in touch with Katherine. That was awesome of you guys and means a lot to me. But don't worry if she tells me she doesn't want to be with me anymore. I understand that there's going to be a lot of changes in her life, so don't worry, I'm not gonna go crazy. I'm just hoping for the best and preparing for the worst. But if we're still talking in November and she still wants to be with me, I'll plan stuff out for graduation and see if she can come down with you guys.

I'm just scared of not graduating and having you guys come down for nothing. I don't want to fail and I don't want to let you guys down. That's why I can't really enjoy this because I'm just still really nervous about the M-16 range.

Oh, there are two guys here from New York; one kid from Flushing, Queens and another from Upstate. Don't worry, I'm not the littlest guy in the group; there's two guys here who weigh about 120 lbs. and they're shorter than me, too. On the road march I had to help one kid out. The drill sergeant was really up his ass. We were going up a rocky hill

and he was just dying out and I felt bad since he asked for
my help. Besides, I couldn't just let him fall behind. But I
got him to the end of the road march.

It sucks seeing people having a hard time with stuff and
other people just ignore them. Plus, the drill sergeants will
yell at them and call them really graphic names. But don't
worry, I haven't been cursed at more than once or twice.
No big thing. The only time I got in trouble was when I
was kicking the crap out of this kid in pugil stick fighting;
I knocked the stick out of his hands and kept hitting him
because I didn't hear the drill sergeants telling me to stop.
So they yelled at me but then let us fight again. It was fun
and don't worry, we don't get hurt.

I like the training but it just sucks not being able to call
people a lot. But that's Basic Training. Take care, I love you
guys and let me know how the family is.

Love,
Mike

"We are very interested to hear what it is like for you undergoing all that training," his parents wrote back a few days later. "We know it must be difficult (well, Dad does for sure) but you can definitely do it, we are certain."

After writing that they were "glad you are not the smallest guy in the place" so he wouldn't be a "large target," Linda and Bob gave their son some relationship advice.

"You sound realistic when it comes to Katherine. We are glad about that. We like Katherine very much also. But at this time in your lives there are so many changes going on and different life paths," they wrote. "So we agree with you. Enjoy your relationship now and whatever happens, happens. Katherine is certainly welcome to come to Georgia with us if she wants.

"Lots of people are asking about you, so you are being missed quite a bit," Linda and Bob wrote in closing. "We are praying that all goes well with the firing range. Don't worry. We repeat, don't worry!"

The next few weeks couldn't have been more eventful for Mike and his fellow army recruits, starting with the gas-chamber training exercise he had previously mentioned as being right around the corner. It involved Mike going inside the chamber and removing his mask and putting it back on exactly as instructed while also holding on to his rifle.

"I did all the stuff they wanted me to do," Mike wrote in a subsequent letter home. "It was fun, but painful."

The constant training exercises, road marches, and physical training tests would wear on almost anyone, especially a northerner not accustomed to dealing with such punishing southern heat in September and beyond. Mike told his parents he was getting used to it, but he never really did. All he could do was hope and pray that some relief from the southwest Georgia humidity would finally come in October, whose arrival he was reminded of when an early Halloween card came from his sister Kelly, attending college at the time in Baltimore.

"I wanted to send candy, but Mommy said you weren't allowed any packages," Kelly wrote to her brother. "I can't come to your graduation because I have an exam, but Dave and I will take you out when you get home. Take care and finish strong!"

At Mike's request, Kelly had made him an MP3 CD full of his favorite songs. While some of it was slower stuff like Billy Joel and Dave Matthews Band, most of it was hard rock and heavy metal like Metallica, Disturbed, System of a Down, Slayer, Judas Priest, Slipknot, Pantera, and AC/DC. The louder the music, the more it helped fire Mike and his fellow recruits up for endless training missions and marches on those humid southwest Georgia days and nights.

Despite all his fears about the M16 test, Mike would qualify in mid-September and move on to training with more advanced weapons. That achievement would lead to the loudest *"Hooah!"* yelled to that point by Mike and his new army buddies.

"We are so glad that the M-16 firing test was a success," Bob and Linda wrote. "We are proud to know that you made sharpshooter. Good work! We hope that you had some fun on your birthday."

He did indeed have some fun, as a thirty-six-hour break coincided with his birthday. Mike wound up attending a Lynyrd Skynyrd concert and going to a Waffle House afterward to try some grits, which was perhaps his first true taste of southern life.

"I had a lot of fun with my battle buddies. Skynyrd put on a good show," Mike wrote to his sister Kelly. "Things here are good, but I am ready to go to my unit. But I do love training.

"Well, I have to cut this short 'cause I have to get ready for a ten-mile road march in the morning. We have to be up at 4:00 a.m.," Mike wrote to his sister in conclusion. "But anyway, wish me luck and you take care of yourself."

Soon after passing the M16 test, Mike wrote to his parents about the next part of his unit's training on September 21, 2006:

> Hey Dad and Mom,
> We go into Blue Phase today. I qualified with the grenade—I got expert. So far, I've shot two machine guns—M249 SAW and M240 Bravo. It was fun. We did an eight-mile road march yesterday, then when we got back into our bay the drill sergeants threw all our stuff around and made a mess. Then they smoked us, meaning we did PT for an hour straight. One kid threw up, which was gross, but we got through the day.
> Dad, you've got to see the M240 Bravo, that thing is awesome. I got to take it apart and put it back together. I was also shooting targets that were 500 meters away.

Thanks for the package. If you can send regular band-aids, me and a couple of my battle buddies could use some. We keep cutting up our hands and two guys already got staph infections.

I miss you guys and love you and I'll try to call this week but I have to call Katherine first because I miss her. Oh, if you talk to her please don't tell her that I'm going to Germany. Don't tell anyone, not even Rob or Jimmy or whoever stops by the house.

Well, I've got to go and shoot a Mark 19 automatic grenade launcher and the best machine gun in the world: the 50 cal (caliber). I can't wait for that—wish me luck!

Love,
Mike

Indeed, Mike had learned that after boot camp graduation in November 2006, he would be joining the Second Battalion, Sixth Infantry Regiment of the US Army's First Armored Division based in Baumholder, Germany. He would start out as a rifleman in Alpha Company serving and training on the US Army garrison known as "the Rock" in western Germany's mountainous Rhineland-Pfalz region. For Mike, the news of his first set of orders came as a big surprise.

Mike was excited for the future and would follow whatever orders the army gave him, but was nevertheless disappointed that his inaugural assignment wouldn't be inside the United States. He had requested Fort Hood in Texas as his first destination, but the army isn't usually concerned with where a young PFC is hoping to go, especially during wartime.

In late 2006, the situation in Iraq was deteriorating so rapidly that the then president George W. Bush was considering a "surge" of more US troops in an attempt to stabilize the country, which was teetering on the brink of an all-out civil war. Afghanistan wasn't in the headlines as much as Iraq at the time, but it still presented huge challenges for political and military leaders five years into the post-9/11 conflict.

Mike knew that deploying to Europe would almost certainly spell the end of his relationship with Katherine, who loved him but would nevertheless be thousands of miles away while surrounded by young men on a large college campus. They were only eighteen, but as his parents had noted, Mike was being mature beyond his years when it came to recognizing that the relationship, while rewarding, almost certainly wouldn't work in the long term.

Katherine took the news of her boyfriend heading to Europe better than Mike thought at first, which was a huge relief. He asked his parents to check in on her in the days and weeks that followed since the number of phone calls he could make while in boot camp at Fort Benning was severely limited.

"Daddy called Katherine up at school on her cell. She told us that you called her," Linda wrote to Mike. "Of course, we understand about love. After all, we have been married 35 years!"

For now, Mike and Katherine would stay together and very much looked forward to seeing each other for the first time after his graduation in November. At long last, the finish line was in sight:

> Hey Mom and Dad,
> Thanks for the ChapStick, I gave some to my battle buddies. We've got one more week of training left then FTX then two weeks of recovery.
>
> This past Saturday we had to take a PT test. I improved. I did 51 push-ups, 63 sit-ups and I ran two miles in 12:15. I think we might have one more PT test but I hope not.
>
> FTX are field training exercises. We have to go out in the field for a few days and sleep outside. The last day of

FTX, we have to march 12 miles with our stuff on and if anyone falls out, you can't graduate. So I'm just a little nervous. I just want to get those crosses, rifles and my blue rope.

Love,
Mike

Before FTX, Mike got another letter from Master Sergeant Jackson:

Mike,
I received your letter today and I was glad to hear from you. If you want me at Benning on Graduation Day, I'll be there. I'll just need to know ASAP if any dates change.

Listen, take care, stay low and go slow but never stop. You can! You will! You must! My motto is "I carried always."

God bless you and all the troops everywhere!
Master Sergeant Jackson

On a crisp fall afternoon in November 2006, PFC Michael Ollis officially became an infantryman in the United States Army. Before graduation, he got one last letter from Katherine, who had written to her boyfriend every day he was in boot camp. Amazingly, Mike had responded to every one of her letters despite being completely exhausted almost every single night:

Can you believe it?
15 weeks of Basic (including that first processing week) and we did it! You were right, the days were long but the weeks were short. Thank you so much for all you did. I'm sure you must have been so tired but I really appreciate you taking the time to write me every day. I can honestly say

getting those letters meant the world to me. Thank you so much.

I love you.

Katherine couldn't attend the graduation because of school commitments, but Mike was thrilled that Master Sergeant Jackson was able to join his parents at Fort Benning for the ceremony. Becoming a soldier in front of the two men most responsible for molding him into an American warrior was the greatest honor of Mike's life to that point.

"You did it, PFC Ollis!" Master Sergeant Jackson said. "I'm proud of you."

When Mike turned to his parents, it was almost impossible not to shed a tear at the culmination of a lifelong journey to follow his dad into the army's enlisted ranks. As he hugged and kissed his mom, Mike made sure to thank her and tell her not to worry. He was only going to Germany, not Iraq or Afghanistan—at least not yet.

Bob knew that Mike would most likely end up on the front lines in one of those countries, or perhaps even both. For now, though, it was time to celebrate an achievement that, as he knew firsthand, his son had worked hard to attain. It wasn't just those fifteen weeks at Fort Benning; it took fifteen years. Since he was two years old, running around his Staten Island neighborhood playing army with toy guns, Mike had been preparing for this moment. On this special fall day—at long last—Mike was an American soldier just like his dad.

"My father thought it was a privilege to serve the country he lives in and now so do I," Mike had written in that student yearbook dedication. Years later, the sentiment Mike originally expressed couldn't have possibly been stronger.

"I did this for you, Dad," Mike said while hugging his father at his graduation.

"No, son, you did this for *you*," Bob said. "You've made us all proud, but this is your day, not mine."

"Thanks, Dad," Mike said before sporting a huge smile. *"Hooah!"*

A few days after the pomp and circumstance of the Fort Benning graduation ceremony, Mike made his first visit home since leaving for basic training. He was greeted by nearly everyone—his parents; Kim; Bill; Kelly and her husband, Dave Manzolillo; countless relatives; Jimmy; Rob; Quaseem; Alanna; Kristen; and perhaps most important to Mike at the time—Katherine. With Mike wearing his shiny new dress uniform, the long-distance couple finally reunited before a memorable hot tub party with friends that night while Bruce Springsteen's "Glory Days" and other favorite classic rock and newer pop songs blasted in the now-famous Ollis backyard.

Mike was also thrilled to hear that their buddy Bolivar had graduated from Marine Corps boot camp as well. He couldn't wait until the two of them had the chance to talk and exchange wild basic training stories.

Best of all, Mike joined Kim and Bill in welcoming their second son, Joseph, on December 13, 2006. He was also able to wish his oldest nephew, William, a happy early third birthday ahead of a January 3, 2007, family celebration that he would be unable to attend.

A few weeks after Mike once again bid farewell to his family and friends and flew over to Europe, his local paper, the *Staten Island Advance,* published an announcement about their newest hometown hero:

Michael Ollis of New Dorp graduated from the US Army Infantry Training Brigade at Fort Benning, Ga., following 14 weeks of training.

He is currently stationed in Baumholder, Germany, with the 1st Armored Division.

Ollis is a 2006 graduate of Michael Petrides High School. He is the son of Robert E. and Linda Ollis.

It was strange for Mike to see his name in print when his parents mailed him the newspaper clipping. All he could do was smile and laugh, as the young soldier figured it was the only time his name would ever be in his local newspaper. Mike couldn't have known how wrong that prediction would end up being.

CHAPTER 4

BROTHERS-IN-ARMS

just want to say thank you for what you are doing. I hope you
come home safe."

It had been only a few years since Mike wrote those words to
American troops who were sent to fight overseas after 9/11. In
2007, the combat boot was on the other foot as Private First Class
Michael Harold Ollis responded to letters mailed to him by a class
at the same school he attended for a decade before becoming a
US Army soldier:

> Dear Mrs. Carr, Mrs. Carola and Class,
> I would like to thank you for all your letters, support for the
> military and your country. Letters like yours are what keeps
> soldiers like me working hard for our country even though
> the job gets stressful and tiring. Mrs. Carr and Mrs. Carola,
> I wish to thank you for letting the students write to me,
> thereby opening up their minds to let them see what we are
> doing in the military.
>
> Class, I would like to answer all your questions and tell
> you about myself and the reason why I serve. My name is
> Private First Class Michael Ollis and I am 19 years old. I

was born and raised in Staten Island. I lived in New Dorp
for 17 years. I have a mom and dad and two older sisters
named Kim and Kelly and one crazy dog named Sydney.
My favorite sport to play is soccer. I've played it all of my life
but I love to watch football, baseball and hockey. My favorite
teams are the New York Giants, New York Mets and the
New York Rangers. I have a lot of favorite movies but if I had
to name one, it would be all of the Star Wars movies. My
favorite hero is Batman. I like the color blue.

I have several reasons why I joined the military. I always
wanted to be a soldier from when I was a kid. It seemed
like a cool thing to do. But when 9/11 happened, I knew
from then on that I was going to be a soldier no matter
what. I enjoy being a soldier and I do not look back from
joining the Army. When times get tough and I miss my
family, I know I'm doing this for them and for our country.

My job in the Army is being an infantryman. My job
will send me into combat when certain problems occur. In
the infantry, my unit trained me to be a Bradley driver and
when I'm not in the Bradley, I am on the ground walking.
My Bradley is an infantry fighting vehicle. It kind of looks
like a tank, but it's made to bring soldiers into battle, to
give them cover and to bring them out of the battle when
the fight gets too dangerous.

I am stationed in Germany. It's a very nice country but
it doesn't compare to the United States. I don't know when
I'll go to Iraq, but it will be sometime soon. I am a little
nervous and also excited. I just want to do the best that I
can and make my family proud.

Well, it was nice writing to all of you. I hope you will
keep in touch.

All the best,
PFC Ollis

Mike had arrived in Baumholder, Germany, in early 2007 and immediately hit the ground running. While he started as a rifleman in Alpha Company, he quickly moved to the mounted section as a driver of the aforementioned M2A2 Bradley infantry fighting vehicle (IFV).

As an IFV driver, he was responsible for the vehicle's maintenance and operation, changing oil, replacing parts, removing engines and transmissions, changing tracks and track pads. Mike's longtime interest in cars and trucks—heavily influenced by his dad taking him to work from a young age to watch him perform maintenance on those *New York Daily News* trucks—clearly helped him land his first job in the US Army.

The Bradley was in almost constant need of repair, and while Mike was in the Rhineland-Pfalz, one could almost always find him in a motor-pool bay working hard on IFVs throughout each week. While stationed at the Rock, Mike was directly responsible for approximately three million dollars' worth of military equipment. What fellow soldiers and commanding officers noticed most, however, was that Mike always seemed to have a smile on his face while hard at work on these massive army vehicles. He truly loved what he was doing.

"This is great!" Mike would often yell while working on one of the massive military vehicles.

In one instance, Mike spotted one of the IFVs leaking all of its fuel in the hull of the passenger compartment just as he was finishing up work for the day. Mike and a group of soldiers then used Dixie cups to remove the fuel by hand. It was no small task, as the huge vehicle carried over 150 gallons of fuel. After working well into the night, Mike and his fellow soldiers were rewarded with a small pizza party thrown by a grateful commanding officer.

In late 2007, Mike moved to what is now called US Army Garrison Bavaria, which is near Germany's border with the Czech Republic. He was stationed at Tower Barracks in Grafenwoehr, which houses thousands of US troops, military families, and civilian contractors.

While at the Grafenwoehr Training Area, Mike and his unit ran drills specifically centered on an upcoming deployment to Iraq, even though they didn't know exactly when it would occur. After thirty straight days of training at Grafenwoehr, Mike earned his official US Army qualifications on the IFV and company and battalion operations. For his outstanding work as an IFV operator, Mike earned his first Army Achievement Medal. It was a good feeling and Mike couldn't wait to tell his parents what he had accomplished.

Mike was then sent back to Baumholder, where he and the rest of Alpha Company conducted mounted and dismounted training and qualifying exercises on the M4 carbine assault rifle, M203 and MK19 grenade launchers, M2.50 caliber, M240 and M249 machine guns. Most important for Mike, he trained heavily on the 25 mm M242 Bushmaster machine gun, which was the main weapon used on the M2A2 Bradley IFV.

This part of army training was even more fun for Mike than boot camp at Fort Benning. All he seemed to be doing in Germany for those few months was shooting guns and blowing things up.

After completing all of his European training, which also included calling for indirect fire, land navigation training, and civil engagement training, Private First Class Michael Ollis was specially selected to become the commander's driver in headquarters platoon. That meant whenever his unit went to Iraq, Mike would be responsible for driving and protecting their commanding officer through the war zone. It was an important responsibility that earned Mike a second Army Achievement Medal for his accomplishments in Germany.

While finishing up his predeployment training at the Joint Multinational Training Center in Hohenfels, Mike found out that in March 2008, he would be heading to Kuwait as part of an advanced deployment team that would receive armored military vehicles at one of the country's naval ports. From there, he would join the rest of his battalion at an American base before heading to Iraq. Before deploying to the Middle East, however, Mike and his soon-to-be battle buddies would get to enjoy some well-deserved time off to explore Europe.

Mike and his new army friends, including two friendly soldiers named Brian Constantino (nicknamed Tino) and Jason Matney, would make the most of their vacation time on the continent. In Germany, they would visit Munich, Nuremberg, Cologne, and Idar-Oberstein. They also visited the Netherlands, Spain, and Italy, where Mike would explore the ancient ruins of Rome.

Way back in second grade at Petrides, young Mikey's teacher had the class make "passports to the world" and list the places they wanted to visit. By age nineteen, Mike had already checked off many of the countries on his list. Getting a chance to see the world at such a young age was one of his favorite things about being an American soldier.

One of the reasons Brian, Jason, and the other soldiers in their small clique liked Mike so much is because he always provided comic relief. As he was with his friends back in Staten Island, Mike—whom they nicknamed Ollie—was the glue that held the group together.

While taking a cruise with his army buddies down the majestic Rhine, Mike suddenly had an idea when the boat stopped in front of a few ancient castles that were just beyond the riverbank. After leading his platoon into a nearby town to buy souvenir toy swords, Mike shouted out one of his first army commands.

"To the castle!" he yelled with his best British accent.

Before his future battle buddies knew it, they were scaling a medieval castle's wall in a scene straight out of *Robin Hood* or *Braveheart*. When they reached the top, the soldiers began sword-fighting with one another as they all laughed and pretended to fall down and die when they got stabbed. In that hilarious moment, Mike probably felt as if he were playing in the street back on Burbank Avenue instead of on the balcony of an ancient European castle.

As in Staten Island, Mike always wanted to have a good time and made others want to do the same. His swordplay wasn't a coping mechanism to deal with the fact that they were about to head to Iraq, as the soldiers were too young and inexperienced to fully anticipate what they were about to get into. They were just a bunch of nineteen- and twenty-year-old guys who wanted to see the world, have a great time, and—perhaps most important— meet some beautiful European women.

The camaraderie between Mike, Tino, Jason, and the other soldiers started to develop on their first base in Germany. They all lived a few doors down from one another, so after work most of the guys would gather in Mike's room to play Xbox, talk about the women in their lives, and sneak in a few beers once the coast was clear of commanding officers. Mike had folding lawn chairs in his room that the guys referred to as "drinking chairs" and would fire up some good mid-2000s rock music on his laptop as he sipped beer and swapped stories with his new friends. The guys hung out so often that they eventually constructed a beer "pyramid" using over one hundred cans of beer that they had consumed together.

Mike's group would sometimes also visit the bars in town even if it meant walking two or three miles to get there. While it was a long trek, they often chose the extra exercise over paying cab fare. If any of the guys were too tipsy to make the long walk home, they could sometimes call an army "courtesy patrol" van to drive them back to their Baumholder base for free. During those rides Mike was at his funniest, especially when he would start bugging the driver by belting out whatever song happened to be playing on the radio.

LEFT: Like his big sisters, young Mike loved to play soccer for their church parish, Our Lady Queen of Peace Church in Staten Island, New York.

BELOW: Mike celebrates Christmas while being held by his oldest sister, Kimberly, and joined by his second big sister, Kelly, at the Ollis family's home in Staten Island's New Dorp neighborhood.

TOP: Mike gets a big hug from his mother, Linda.

ABOVE: A future soldier salutes in front of a US Army vehicle while visiting a museum.

RIGHT: Mike designed this 9/11–inspired artwork on his school computer for a class project.

TOP: Mike participates in a flag-folding ceremony during his time in the US Air Force JROTC program at the Michael J. Petrides School in Staten Island.

MIDDLE: Mike holds his nephew William Loschiavo while joined by friends Kristen Strine (left) and Alanna Saunders (right) at the Ollis family home before the 2006 senior prom.

BOTTOM: Mike loved hosting parties with his friends in his parents' back porch screen house, especially after joining the army and coming home on leave.

TOP: Mike stands proudly beside his JROTC commanding officer, US Air Force Master Sergeant Peter Jackson, after graduating from boot camp at Fort Benning (now Fort Moore) in Georgia in November 2006.

BOTTOM: Mike and his fellow soldiers hand out soccer balls to children in Iraq in 2008.

Mike poses in front of camels during his combat deployment to Iraq.

LEFT: Mike is overcome with emotion while visiting the Auschwitz-Birkenau former Nazi concentration and extermination camp during a 2009 trip to Poland.

RIGHT: Mike pins the Bronze Star medal on his father, Vietnam War veteran Bob Ollis.

Mike celebrates Oktoberfest in Germany with US Army
buddies Brian Constantino, Jason Matney, and Amy Matney.

Mike stands in front of a helicopter during his first combat deployment to Afghanistan.

TOP: An explosion at an unknown location in Afghanistan that was photographed and posted to Facebook by Mike.

MIDDLE: Mike carries his grenade launcher, grenades, and other heavy gear on a hot day in Afghanistan.

LEFT: The terrifying aftermath of the enemy IED attack on a small ANA base in Sangsar, Afghanistan, on December 12, 2010. While the image is blurry, the soldier standing and pointing atop the rubble is believed to be Mike. *Courtesy: Roy Patterson*

ABOVE: The US Army Ranger tab is pinned to Mike's shoulder by his friend Jason Matney upon graduating from Ranger School at Fort Benning on July 12, 2012.

LEFT: Mike holds out the US Army Ranger flag during a post-graduation visit home.

LEFT: Kim, Kelly, and Mike pose during a family dinner at Henny's Steakhouse in Staten Island while he was home on leave.

BELOW: Close friends Rob Hemsworth, Jimmy Carter, Quaseem Pipkin, Mike, Bolivar Flores, and Melanie Binder ride the Staten Island Ferry to Manhattan in 2012.

Mike attends his parents' fortieth wedding anniversary celebration at Fort Wadsworth on the New York Harbor in 2012. Left to right: Dave Manzolillo (brother-in-law), Kelly, Ava Manzolillo (niece), Bob, Linda, Mike, Kimberly, Thomas Loschiavo (nephew), Bill Loschiavo (brother-in-law), Joseph Loschiavo (nephew), and William Loschiavo (nephew).

Joseph, William, Uncle Mike, Matthew, and Ava hang out at the Ollis family house in New Dorp.

TOP: Mike and his dad visit the Vietnam Veterans Memorial in Washington.

MIDDLE: Mike becomes godfather to his nephew Matthew at the Parish of St. Clement and St. Michael in Staten Island's Mariners Harbor shortly before leaving for his third combat deployment. To Mike's right is his brother-in-law Dave's sister, Lori Manzolillo.

BOTTOM: Mike flies back to Afghanistan to start his third and final combat deployment.

TOP: Mike works inside his US Army vehicle while serving in Afghanistan in 2013.

MIDDLE: A photo posted by Mike to Facebook showing his and other army vehicles navigating Afghanistan's harsh terrain.

BOTTOM: Mike salutes the American flag during his February 2013 reenlistment ceremony in Afghanistan.

ABOVE: Mike puts his weapon on his back while showing off a Staten Island Biker's Association patch while deployed to Afghanistan in 2013.

BELOW: Polish troops guard FOB Ghazni's breached perimeter wall during the enemy attack on August 28, 2013. *Courtesy: Polish Land Forces*

US Army soldiers carry the flag-draped casket of Staff Sergeant Michael Ollis during a dignified transfer ceremony at Dover Air Force Base in Delaware on August 31, 2013. *Courtesy: US Air Force/David Tucker*

Kelly, Kim, and Bill meet the soldier whom Mike saved—Polish Second Lieutenant Karol Cierpica—for the first time at the Polish Consulate in New York on November 12, 2013. *Courtesy: Consulate General of the Republic of Poland in New York*

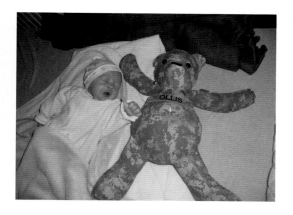

TOP: Newborn baby Michael Cierpica lies next to a teddy bear made out of Mike's army fatigues. *Courtesy: Cierpica family*

MIDDLE: US Army soldiers including one of Mike's best friends, Sergeant First Class Brian Schnell (rear), admire a painting of Mike and a shadow box containing some of his awards and personal items during a rededication ceremony for the Staff Sergeant Michael H. Ollis Weapons Training Center at New York's Fort Drum on September 26, 2019. *Courtesy: Fort Drum Garrison Public Affairs/Mike Strasser*

BOTTOM: US Army General James McConville presents Mike's posthumous Distinguished Service Cross to Linda and Bob at the SSG Michael Ollis VFW Post 9587 on June 8, 2019. *Courtesy: US Army/Sergeant Jerod Hathaway*

ABOVE LEFT: Karol and Bob join hands at the Distinguished Service Cross ceremony. *Courtesy: US Army/Sergeant Jerod Hathaway*

ABOVE RIGHT: The Ollis-class ferry *MV SSG Michael H. Ollis* sails between the St. George Terminal in Staten Island and Whitehall Terminal in lower Manhattan. The *Ollis* made its maiden voyage on February 14, 2022. *Courtesy: New York City Department of Transportation*

BELOW: The SSG Michael Ollis sculpture and Memorial Plaza now graces the very grounds that Mike once walked at the Michael J. Petrides School in Staten Island. *Courtesy: Hanlon Sculpture Studio*

One of the group's most epic trips before heading to Iraq was to the historic city of Munich to experience their first authentic German Oktoberfest. It was a completely different environment from a previous trip to Keukenhof, Holland, where they mostly looked at massive gardens of flowers and did what Mike jokingly called "married-type stuff." In Munich, the German beer was flowing and the women were some of the most gorgeous they had ever seen. For the most part, they were also extremely friendly to American visitors.

Mike and Katherine had slowly drifted apart after he went to Europe and she stayed at college. As is the case with many long-distance couples—especially in the military—they eventually broke up. They did, however, manage to remain friends and would still occasionally check in with each other in subsequent years.

While breaking up with his high school sweetheart was painful, Mike—as evidenced by prior conversations with his parents and others—knew deep down that the romance almost certainly wouldn't pan out. Going to Germany and then Iraq made it too tough to stay in close touch, especially at a time before everyone had smartphones with readily available video-call apps.

After completing that brief March 2008 stint at the Kuwaiti naval port, Mike joined the rest of his battalion at Camp Buehring in the northwestern part of the country. Seeing the bright Middle Eastern sand for the first time and feeling the searing desert heat was something no training exercise could have ever prepared Mike for. He was a long way from Staten Island, but was nevertheless happy and content. After all, Mike was doing exactly what he'd always wanted to do alongside a close-knit group of friends who had quickly become his brothers-in-arms.

Shortly before leaving for Kuwait and then Iraq, Mike got a reply to his letter back home from one of the young students at Petrides. It was a card written on red construction paper that included a picture the boy had drawn of the American flag:

Dear PFC Ollis,

I am happy you like "Star Wars," the New York Giants, the New York Mets and the New York Rangers. I like those teams and those movies also.

Will you be going into war soon? Will your friends be fighting with you? How many soldiers are in your squad? Would you run into enemy fire to save a soldier?

Happy Valentine's Day. I hope you get a higher rank soon. I also hope you get to fight with your friends.

From,
Paul W.

CHAPTER 5

OLLIE'S GOT IT

Hey guys," Mike wrote on what looked like a torn-off section of a UPS or Amazon package. "I got this post card from an MRE [meal ready to eat] box."

The 2008 post card was mailed by the deployed American soldier from Combat Outpost (COP) Carver in Salman Pak, Iraq, which is about fifteen miles southeast of Baghdad. It was addressed from Mike to his parents.

"I'm in the back of my Bradley just chilling," he wrote. "We've been driving all day. I've been dropping off troops so they can clear houses.

"It's been a hot day. It's around 90 degrees but it's not too bad," Mike continued. "I figured I'd write because the post card looks cool and I just wanted to say hello. Love, Mike."

Private First Class Michael Ollis and the rest of the Second Battalion, Sixth Infantry Regiment's Alpha Company started their combat deployment in April 2008, which wound up becoming the deadliest month of that year for US troops in Iraq. According to icasualties.org, fifty-two American service members lost their lives in the war-torn country that April. Many more were wounded.

Five years after American-led forces deposed Saddam Hussein's regime and tore down a large statue of the Iraqi dictator, the US military was still desperately trying to win the war. President George W. Bush's Iraq troop "surge," which was led by US Army General David Petraeus, was in its second year as US service members fought hard to secure Baghdad and the even more volatile Anbar Province. Results thus far were mixed, although General Petraeus's innovative counterinsurgency strategy was beginning to show clear signs of success.

"I think everybody recognizes that there has been progress in the security arena over the course of the last six to eight months," General Petraeus told CBS News on March 19, 2008.

The Iraq War's commanding general testified before the Senate Armed Services Committee on April 8, 2008, just as Mike and his fellow soldiers were starting their mission:

> Since Ambassador [Ryan] Crocker and I appeared before you seven months ago, there has been significant but uneven security progress in Iraq. Since September, levels of violence and civilian deaths have been reduced substantially. Al Qaeda in Iraq and a number of other extremist elements have been dealt serious blows. The capabilities of Iraqi security force elements have grown, and there has been noteworthy involvement of local Iraqis and local security.
>
> Nonetheless, the situation in certain areas is still unsatisfactory, and innumerable challenges remain. Moreover, as events in the past two weeks have reminded us, and as I have repeatedly cautioned, the progress made since last spring is fragile and reversible. Still, security in Iraq is better than it was when Ambassador Crocker and I reported to you last September, and it is significantly better than it was 15 months ago when Iraq was on the brink of civil

war and the decision was made to deploy additional forces to Iraq.

The year 2008 marked another presidential election, which meant that political divisions at home over the Iraq War had reached a fever pitch. A USA Today/Gallup poll conducted between April 18–20, 2008, found that 63 percent of Americans believed that the 2003 invasion of Iraq was a mistake. Democratic politicians—including Senator Joe Biden, who would become Senator Barack Obama's running mate later that year—pushed back at General Petraeus throughout his testimony before the Senate Foreign Relations Committee later on that same day.

"You need to do much more than inform the Congress," said Senator Biden, as quoted by The New York Times. "You need the permission of the Congress if you're going to bind the next president of the United States in anything you agree to."

Mike and his fellow US Army infantry soldiers in Salman Pak, Iraq, were almost certainly not following the daily political posturing back home. Their job was working with locals to help identify Iraqi insurgents while trying to assure them that the US military was on their side.

The soldiers started by screening people who seemingly blended into the civilian population in order to look for links to those who were helping fund and support insurgent groups. While most Iraqi civilians wanted peace, some were still helping the insurgents undermine and attack the new Iraqi government. Mike and his company would also occasionally be tasked with hunting down, arresting, and fighting against al Qaeda in Iraq and other terrorist groups.

It was in Iraq where Mike first felt the awesome responsibility of having another person's life in his hands. Even for a calm, happy-go-lucky guy like Mike, worrying about the safety of his fellow soldiers would often keep him up at night. Failing at his job would mean that one or more of his buddies could get wounded or killed. That sobering reality meant that Mike had to be at his best every single day during a marathon fifteen-month deployment at the height of the Iraq War.

To a young soldier from Staten Island, suddenly finding himself in the cradle of civilization couldn't have been more jarring or surreal. Salman Pak included ruins from ancient cities like Ctesiphon, which was the capital of Persia's Sasanian Empire from AD 226 to 637. *Stars and Stripes* correspondent John Vandiver described what it was like for soldiers in Mike's Second Battalion, Sixth Infantry Regiment to live and work in the historic city in a report filed on May 30, 2008:

> When the soldiers of Task Force 2–6 Infantry patrol through the market places of downtown Salman Pak, a city 15 miles southeast of Baghdad, they operate under the shadow of one of the world's great landmarks.
>
> At the edge of town stands the Arch of Ctesiphon, which is reported to be the world's oldest free-standing arch.
>
> Constructed in 400, it is the only remaining structure of the city of Ctesiphon, which was the largest city in the world during the sixth century. The city also was mentioned in the biblical Book of Ezra under the name Casphia.
>
> On a recent patrol of downtown, the 2–6 soldiers made a stop at the site, which is guarded by members of the Iraqi army.
>
> At one time, the city of Salman Pak was a tourist hub for Baghdad's elite, with the arch serving as a top attraction. After years of violence and conflict it remains to be

seen whether the city will again serve as a weekend get-away spot.

Mike and his battle buddies had read about the history of Salman Pak and its once-bustling streets along the Tigris River that were said to resemble the French Riviera. After their first few weeks on patrol, the soldiers knew they were definitely not serving in a tourist destination. The tragic events of June 23, 2008, further underscored the reality of the danger the soldiers would be facing on a daily basis.

On that particular day, Alpha Company was tasked with cordoning off a government building where a seemingly routine meeting between US and Iraqi officials was taking place. Like most typical days, the soldiers in Mike's company would spend a few hours either inside their vehicles or patrolling on foot to make sure the site remained secure. Once the meeting was over, they would pack up and go back to their base.

Right as Alpha Company's convoy returned to COP Carver, several soldiers heard gunshots as they disembarked from their vehicles. The sounds were coming from an area that was seemingly very close to the government building they had just finished guarding. Within a few moments, the soldiers remounted and began racing back to town in case their support was needed during a potentially prolonged firefight. They were too late.

"A US-allied Iraqi council member sprayed American troops with gunfire Monday, killing two soldiers and wounding three and an interpreter, Iraqi authorities and witnesses said," Mohammed Al Dulaimy and Hannah Allam reported for the McClatchy wire service the next day. "The attack occurred minutes after they emerged from a weekly joint meeting on reconstruction in this volatile town southeast of Baghdad."

Mike and his fellow soldiers watched in silence as the wounded were carried in on stretchers to receive treatment at COP Carver's aid station. They were then medevacked on UH-60 Black Hawk helicopters to the much larger Camp Liberty's hospital in Baghdad. It was a solemn, eye-opening experience for Mike and everyone who witnessed those difficult moments.

As they would later find out, the attack took the lives of US Army Captain Gregory Dalessio, a thirty-year-old soldier from Cherry Hill, New Jersey, and Private First Class Bryan Thomas, twenty-two, from Lake Charles, Louisiana. Both were members of Mike's battalion who had deployed to Iraq from Baumholder, Germany.

The very combat outpost Mike was stationed on was named after a fallen US Army soldier, in fact. Quickly built as part of General Petraeus's strategy to shift US troops to small bases spread all across the battlefield, COP Carver was named for a nineteen-year-old departed warrior named PFC Cody Carver. He was the same age as Mike when he made the ultimate sacrifice during an October 30, 2007, enemy improvised explosive device (IED) attack, which made Cody's story even more relatable to the young members of Alpha Company.

"He was barely [in Iraq] for thirty days," the fallen soldier's mother, Pamela Carver, told the *Tulsa World* in 2007. "We were very proud of what he was doing. He had just received an expert marksmanship award, too. He was a good soldier and a really good person."

Knowing that there were talented young soldiers like PFC Carver who tragically didn't make it through the first month of their deployment made the mission facing Mike and his battle buddies even more daunting. For approximately 450 straight days, every single member of Mike's company would wake up wondering if that given morning would wind up being their last. It's a feeling that only someone who's experienced war can truly understand.

Less than two months before Mike and his fellow soldiers arrived in Iraq, Reuters reporter Tim Cocks vividly described what conditions were like for Americans stationed in Salman Pak. His report was filed back on February 19, 2008, while construction work on COP Carver was still being completed:

> On a patch of Iraqi desert flanked by palm trees, US soldiers erect concrete blast walls and saw wooden planks to make cabins. Out front, a gunner tests his mortar launcher, firing a round into an empty field.
>
> The soldiers are building the latest US combat outpost in Iraq, a tactical shift begun a year ago to move troops off their relatively safe, sprawling bases and into small garrisons in and around the country's dangerous neighborhoods and towns.
>
> The town of Salman Pak, 45 km [25 miles] south of Baghdad, had long been a haven for al Qaeda, whose bombers used it as a springboard to launch car bomb attacks on Baghdad.

The reporter outlined plans to reinforce and improve COP Carver ahead of Mike's company and other soldiers arriving in the weeks and months ahead:

> "The greatest threat is the IED," said Lieutenant-Colonel Jack Marr, a battalion commander in the area. "It's science: drive less, less opportunity to be hit by an IED. We wanted to import that success, which is what led us to building Carver."
>
> Like other outposts, called COPs by the military, the new one takes the name of a soldier killed in battle. Private Cody Carver, 19, died when his tank hit an IED on a Salman Pak road.
>
> With a just a perimeter fence, wood cabins, a row of

tents and cold showers, the week-old camp is basic. Soldiers here hope that within a month, it will look like nearby COP Cahill.

There, tents are heated and so is water, the canteen serves hot meals. There is a gym, a firing range, a TV in the dining room, Internet and table tennis—comforts they eventually got after months sleeping in cold, spider-infested fields.

Mike may not have had to sleep in any spider-infested fields, but conditions at COP Carver were still far from ideal when his company arrived. Mike, Brian Constantino, Jason Matney, and their battle buddies were assigned to live in thirty-foot containers that were stacked around in different areas of the relatively small, T-walled COP, which was located between farmland and the main city.

There was still no base dining facility, which meant that their first task upon arrival was to build one. Mike and his company would also construct a small gym and morale, welfare, and recreation (MWR) hall, where they would eventually be able to get online with an extremely slow internet connection. Everything was essentially built from scratch, including the centralized housing units the soldiers would construct so they could finally move out of those stacked containers and into more traditional rooms.

During the first six months of their deployment, the routine became consistent: the soldiers would wake up, go on a mission, and then do some COP construction work before hitting the gym. While US troops deployed to Iraq in 2008 didn't usually sleep comfortably as they listened to the gunfire and explosions that often surrounded them, the soldiers in Mike's company might have been an exception. They were so exhausted by the evening hours that they usually slept like babies.

When the soldiers got some rare downtime, Mike's room was

usually the gathering spot, just as it had been when they were stationed in Germany. There, they would fire up the Xbox, watch movies, and openly fantasize about reuniting with their respective love interests upon getting back home.

Mike still served as the company's comic relief, especially when he had his shirt off. He had been born with a minor congenital deformity called pectus excavatum, which essentially meant that he had an indent in the center of his chest. While it was not a severe case that doctors thought would interfere with his heart or lungs, Mike's "sunken chest" was definitely noticeable and a long-running source of jokes among friends both back home and in the army.

"Yo Ollie, I wish I could eat my breakfast that way," Tino said to Mike one morning as they lay in their respective cots playing video games before heading out for the day's mission. Mike was lying on his back and using the indent in his chest to hold and balance his bowl of cereal.

When they went out drinking together in Germany, Mike would sometimes take off his shirt and let the local ladies do shots of liquor from that unique spot in his chest. It was almost always the highlight of a given night of partying. He often did the same thing during those epic backyard parties back home in Staten Island.

As Mike had known since his JROTC days, there was a time to laugh and a time to get serious. When his squad left COP Carver each morning, Mike suddenly transformed from the company clown to a serious soldier in the heat of battle. After all, lives were on the line, including his own.

Whenever there was a problem or unexpected turn of events, everyone in the company—from commanding officers on down— knew they could depend on Mike. Whether it was a quick repair needed for one of the vehicles, issues with the COP's infrastructure, or even the internet going down, most would immediately look to Mike with full confidence that he could fix it.

"Don't worry," soldiers on COP Carver would often say, "Ollie's got it."

Mike's fierce but measured approach to his job and careful attention to detail eventually earned him a promotion. Ahead of his peers, Mike was promoted to the rank of specialist a few months into their first deployment. He couldn't wait to tell his mom and dad.

Upon his promotion, Specialist Ollis was positioned as a fire team leader, which meant that he was responsible for the welfare, fitness, morale, and discipline of a four-man team. He was also their primary instructor and advisor in matters of tactics, personnel management, and leadership development. Mike embraced the additional responsibilities, but not because he could sometimes tell members of his team what to do. He genuinely wanted to help them become better soldiers while also continuing to learn himself.

Mike's most important job throughout the deployment was being the commander's driver. While he was involved in hundreds of combat patrols throughout his fifteen months in Iraq, Mike always yearned to be on foot like Tino, Jason, and his other battle buddies. He was usually following close by, but as a matter of protocol the commanding officer was almost always positioned in the rear of a given patrol or battle. Even though IEDs still presented a huge threat for anyone driving around Iraq at the time, the threat wasn't as great as being on foot.

After a firefight one day northeast of Baghdad in Diyala, Mike was already back at COP Carver eagerly waiting to talk to Tino and Jason about the mission. While he understood the importance of being the commander's driver and right-hand man, especially if his boss's life was ever in danger, it occasionally frustrated Mike not to be fighting side by side every day with his infantry brothers-in-arms.

Mike also sometimes went on different missions from his friends since the commander's presence was often essential to meetings with Iraqi officials. Whether it was helping set up elections or key leader-engagement meetings designed to build trust between the Americans and local leaders, Mike was almost always on-site to drive and protect the commander.

One day in Salman Pak, Mike was doing his usual job when a disagreement erupted between two dueling Iraqi factions. Before he knew it, the local officials were firing AK-47s at one another in the middle of the town.

It was the first time Mike believed the commander's life might actually be in danger, which meant that his training kicked in before the officer he was protecting could blink an eye. With his weapon drawn, Mike hastily got the commander into the Bradley IFV and roared back to their base, ready to take out anyone who might dare fire a shot or threaten their vehicle.

Still, being assigned to the headquarters section to protect the commander meant that Mike missed out on almost every other firefight during the deployment. While Mike wasn't chasing glory in Iraq or the army as a whole, he didn't enlist only to be someone's driver. He wanted to do more.

Mike did eventually figure out one way to get off the COP and into the elements a bit more often. A few months into the deployment, Mike called home and asked his parents to round up as many soccer balls as they could find on the shelves of stores in and around Staten Island.

During his long IFV drives around Salman Pak, Baghdad, and elsewhere, Mike would often notice children sitting around the war-torn streets with nothing to do. Knowing full well that soccer was by far a favorite pastime for Iraqis and also his sport of choice while growing up, Mike thought it would be a great idea to get soccer balls into the hands (and feet) of as many Iraqi kids as possible. As Mike anticipated, since it fit in so well with the Petraeus strategy of building camaraderie with the Iraqi people, his proposed soccer trips were usually approved.

Handing out soccer balls to Iraqi children was the single biggest highlight of the deployment for Mike, who was willing to risk his life to brighten their days. At any given moment, a parent or even a child in the crowd could have pulled out a weapon or blown themselves up. It was just the reality of those troubled times in Iraq, where al Qaeda and other terrorists would often blackmail terrified civilians into doing their murderous deeds. Luckily for Mike, he did not encounter any violence during the soccer-ball-handout trips.

While conditions were slowly improving in the areas surrounding COP Carver, they nevertheless remained extremely dangerous throughout Mike's fifteen-month deployment. On September 23, 2008, US Army First Lieutenant Thomas Brown was shot dead while on a dismounted patrol in Salman Pak. The twenty-six-year-old officer lived in the Washington, D.C., suburb of Burke, Virginia, and had also trained at Baumholder and Fort Benning as a member of Mike's battalion. He was only a few weeks away from going on leave.

Despite the pain of each and every American death, the latter portion of Mike's deployment did thankfully produce some of the lowest casualty numbers of the war to that point. The twenty-five US service member deaths that month were down from seventy the previous September, according to icasualties.org. In March 2009, the number dropped to single digits for the first time since the initial invasion six years earlier. The Petraeus strategy—and the hard work by countless hardworking soldiers, airmen, sailors, and marines—had clearly paid dividends in Iraq, as evidenced by President Barack Obama's subsequent decision to put the general in charge of the faltering US-led war in Afghanistan.

For Mike and the young men of Alpha Company, however, Iraq was not only their first overseas adventure as American soldiers but also the longest grind they would ever experience in uniform. Fifteen consecutive months in a volatile place like Salman Pak in 2008 would test the mettle of even the most seasoned war fighter.

That's why in August 2008—about five months before leaving office—President Bush reduced deployments for US Army soldiers serving in Iraq to twelve months. That didn't apply to Mike's company since they had started their deployment in April.

"Our nation owes a special thanks to the soldiers and families who have supported this extended deployment," President Bush said at the White House. "We owe a special thanks to all who served in the cause for freedom in Iraq."

By the time Mike, Tino, Jason, and their fellow soldiers departed Salman Pak, they were truly brothers-in-arms. They went to war as young infantry grunts and left Iraq as leaders.

In Mike's case, he also left as a sergeant, having been promoted ahead of his peers for a second time in just fifteen months. Seven years after writing "I want to be a sergeant" in the "All About Me" assignment he completed as a thirteen-year-old student at Petrides, Mike's dream had finally come true. Even more meaningful to Mike was that he had achieved the same rank as his father.

On June 13, 2009, US Army Sergeant Michael Ollis received a hero's welcome upon returning to his New Dorp neighborhood. He also got to see his name in the newspaper for a second time when Mark Stein of the *Staten Island Advance* covered his homecoming party, which was of course thrown in the Ollis family's beloved backyard:

> What's better than coming home from a tour of duty in Iraq than spending time at home with friends and family, along with a few cold ones?
>
> Nothing.
>
> After over a year in Iraq, Ollis, a New Dorp resident, was treated to a party on June 13 with his closest companions.
>
> "The party was a great time," he said. "It rained on us, but it didn't stop us from partying."

When asked what it's like to be back, Ollis replied: "Little things change here and there, but it's good seeing the family and friends."

The dedicated 20-year-old has followed in the footsteps of a long line of proud Americans: His father and grandfather both served time in the US Army.

Ollis didn't plan to stay idle long, though.

"Ready to head to work though," he said, describing how he'll be returning to his base in Germany before heading to Fort Campbell in Kentucky.

Regarding his tour in Iraq, Ollis said: "You had your good days and you had your bad days. It was a good experience, I feel."

After the party, Mike sat down next to his dad in the family's screened-in backyard porch.

"How did it feel to go over there and get the bad guys?" Bob asked his son.

"Oh, Pop," Mike said softly. "You can't hate everybody. There's bad apples, for sure, but not all of the people there were bad."

As Mike went on to tell his father about handing out soccer balls to those Iraqi kids or meeting local leaders who actually wanted to help their people and find peace, Bob had an epiphany that had eluded him since he was seriously wounded by shrapnel in Hue City, Vietnam, on February 29, 1968. Since that harrowing night, he had felt increasing anger toward the Vietnamese over the deaths of his fellow soldiers and his own physical and emotional wounds.

During that consequential father-son moment, Mike helped Bob heal from a war fought four decades earlier.

"You're right, Michael. Come to think of it, the Vietnamese people I met over there weren't all bad," he told his son. "I shouldn't dislike them."

Four months later, Bob Ollis received the Bronze Star at age sixty-one for braving enemy fire while attempting to save the life of a wounded soldier who wound up passing away later in the rescue effort. Amisha Padnani of the *Staten Island Advance* covered the ceremony, which included Mike pinning the Bronze Star on his father's tan jacket:

> "It was nice," [Bob] said. "But the bitter part was why I got it. I would have given up this award to have this guy still be alive."
>
> Still, getting the award was a symbol not only of Ollis' actions, but of how hard his father-in-law, who also served in the Army, had fought to protect his country in the Battle of the Bulge and all of the experiences his own son, Michael, has gone through in Iraq.
>
> Michael said yesterday that it was his father's words that inspired him join the Army.
>
> "It was mostly the stories that he told me and the pictures that I've seen," he said. "It was an emotional experience and it was an honor to pin him."

After the ceremony, Mike gave his dad a hug.

"I'm proud of you, Pop," he said.

"Thank you, Michael," Bob said while embracing his only son. "But it's me that's proud of you."

CHAPTER 6

EUROPEAN VACATION

I think we should start heading back," said Mike's fellow Iraq War veteran, Brian "Tino" Constantino, in late 2009.

Mike, Tino, and a small group of American soldiers were busy climbing a tall mountain as heavy winds began to whip ahead of a high-altitude snowstorm. They were not equipped with GPS devices and were wearing sweatshirts instead of winter coats. The few candy bars they'd brought with them were long gone and only half a bottle of Gatorade remained between them. To put it generously, they were ill-equipped to ride out an unexpected snowstorm.

The soldiers were not scaling a cliff in Afghanistan. Instead, they found themselves in the Swiss Alps, where they were supposed to be enjoying a European vacation between combat deployments.

"Yeah, Tino, this is not good," Mike said after feeling the high winds and seeing the ominous clouds on the soaring horizon.

To make matters worse, the overly ambitious group of twenty- and twenty-one-year-olds didn't bring any climbing gear and were using a preexisting ladder to scale the cliff. As the winds got heavier, the one and only thing the seasoned combat veterans could lean on was their military training. For years, the army had taught them to excel under even the most challenging conditions, whether war- or weather-related.

At one point, Mike felt his grip on the shaky ladder begin to slip. He had never been up that high or dealt with such ferocious winds, even during sandstorms in Iraq. For a few moments, he worried that he would not die as an American soldier doing his duty but as a dumb kid who took a completely unnecessary risk while on vacation.

The group was fortunate to make it safely down from the mountain, but when they did, they knew that hiking back to the Swiss tourist town of Interlaken was no longer an option. The high-altitude snow would reach the ground as cold, heavy rain, which posed very real risks of hypothermia or even drowning since they had to use the Aare River to guide them back to civilization.

Calculating the time it took them to hike out to the mountains and adding an extra hour for harsh weather conditions, Mike estimated that it would take the group four hours to reach Interlaken—*if* everyone ran.

What started as an impulsive trek into the majestic mountains of Switzerland had quickly devolved into a life-threatening conundrum. For Mike, it was more dangerous than most of the threats he had faced in Iraq.

"And I ran—I ran so far away," Mike sang, channeling a famous '80s pop song by A Flock of Seagulls as he and his fellow soldiers tried to outrun the storm rolling in from the Alps.

For approximately four hours, Mike, Tino, and the rest of the group trudged through wet, cold terrain and finally made it back to the dry clothes, hot chocolate, fireplaces, and warm showers that awaited them at the Interlaken hotel. By the time they arrived, the soldiers were hungry, thirsty, exhausted, and felt as if their soaking-wet feet had completely frozen.

"I guess that wasn't such a good idea," a shaking Tino said with a smile.

After everyone nodded in embarrassment while drinking hot cocoa and clutching their blankets, Mike delivered his usual comic relief.

"So, guys, how are we going to try to kill ourselves tomorrow?" he said, sending his fellow soldiers into fits of laughter.

In that hilarious moment, it would have been hard to convince any of the soldiers that the next day of their Swiss vacation would wind up being even more perilous. That's exactly what happened, though, when the group shook off the cobwebs and decided to go whitewater rafting.

Before heading out on the river, a tour guide told the soldiers that someone had drowned two weeks earlier and the area had just reopened for rafting. The water level was still higher than normal, especially after the previous day's storm, but nevertheless deemed to be below the danger threshold.

Even though they were wearing thick wetsuits, the glacier-chilled water still made the river extremely cold. It didn't take more than a few minutes navigating the rapids for the soldiers to experience conditions that were just as frigid as the day before.

It all started when their raft ripped around a turn and hit a thick, bushy tree that had recently snapped. The trunk was about chest level when it struck Mike, Tino, and the other guys so hard that it knocked all of them off the raft. Even the group's experienced tour guide found himself struggling to swim through the freezing waters.

Hypothermia was far from their biggest concern. The fierce rapids soon pulled everyone underwater while their raft was wrapped around the tree. The water was not only cold but also extremely thick and muddy from the recent runoff. Once again, their lives were at risk.

Everyone's first instinct was to swim back to the boat and try to free it from the fallen tree. It was a mistake that led to several soldiers getting stuck underneath the raft, which was also being obstructed by a large bush on the riverbank. The bush, tree, and raging rapids caused the raft to flip upside down and right side up again within the span of a few seconds. Before anyone could blink, one soldier was trapped under the raft.

Realizing that his friend was about to drown, Mike sprung to action before Tino or the tour guide could react. Braving the harrowing conditions, he pushed through the raging muck, grabbed his friend by the shoulders, and held on even tighter than he had on that mountain ladder the previous day. After pulling him away from the raft, Mike got behind his friend and gave him a boost to climb up and over the bush so he could catch his breath on the riverbank. Mike had just saved his life.

There was no time to relax once Tino told everyone that another friend had become trapped. This time, the soldiers and tour guide worked together to pull him to safety.

Even though he had just spent fifteen months in Iraq, Mike never knew what it truly felt like to save someone's life until that second freezing, frightening day in Switzerland. He knew it was nothing to brag about, however, and never even shared the story except when he joked around about the trip with the guys who were there. After all, why couldn't they just enjoy a vacation like everyone else instead of putting themselves in grave danger?

"We all made it back from Iraq with our arms, legs, fingers, and toes," Brian said in jest. "Yet here we are almost dying our first two days in Switzerland?"

While the group did go skydiving the next day, nothing went wrong and everyone had a great time. The soldiers would later joke that skydiving was by far the safest thing they did during their memorable Swiss vacation.

The group took some other fun and much less dangerous trips around Europe, including to Austria to see the historic city of

Salzburg and a village that—at the time—carried a unique name. When Mike, Tino, and the other guys visited, it was still called Fucking, which they found hilarious for obvious reasons.

"Everyone wants to come here. We can't figure out why!" locals kept telling Mike and his friends as they howled with laughter while barhopping in the Austrian village, which would later change its name to Fugging.

The mood during another chapter of their European travels couldn't have been in starker contrast to their Fucking visit. While touring Poland, the soldiers decided to stop at the Auschwitz concentration camp to pay their respects to Holocaust victims and learn more about the atrocities perpetrated by Adolf Hitler's Nazi regime before and during World War II.

While walking under the death camp's infamous "Arbeit Macht Frei" (German for "work sets you free") entrance sign—which wound up being stolen, vandalized, and recovered a few months later—Mike felt agony for the victims. He also felt immense pride that he was now wearing the uniform of the same US Army that had helped liberate millions of Holocaust victims and bring their jailers and killers to justice. While that day in Poland was painful, Mike would carry those few hours in Auschwitz with him for the rest of his life.

Now a sergeant in the Second Battalion of the 502nd Infantry "Renegades" Regiment of the US Army's legendary 101st Airborne Division, Mike would head to Fort Campbell near Kentucky's border with Tennessee after leaving Europe. From late 2009 to mid-2010, he would earn his Air Assault wings from the army's Sabalauski Air Assault School and subsequently be assigned to Bravo Company as a fire team leader. From there, Mike would go to Fort Polk in Louisiana to train for an upcoming deployment to the southern Afghanistan hotspot of Kandahar.

Similar to the heroes of World War II, Mike firmly believed that he was headed to Afghanistan to defend the defenseless and bring evildoers to justice. After all, it was his city and country that had been attacked on September 11, 2001.

Like so many New Yorkers who had deployed to Afghanistan in the eight-plus years since 9/11, America's war on terrorism was personal for Sergeant Michael Ollis. No matter what challenges lay ahead, he would never give up until the mission was complete.

CHAPTER 7

STRIKE FORCE

For the second time in his still-young military career, Mike was part of a US troop "surge" ordered by the commander in chief and overseen by General David Petraeus. President Barack Obama had announced the surge in the hopes of turning around the war in Afghanistan, which had started just over a month after 9/11 and been "forgotten"—as Obama had argued while the Democratic candidate for president—due to his Republican predecessor's subsequent war in Iraq.

Mike and his unit arrived in one of the war's most violent theaters—the southernmost Kandahar Province—squarely in the middle of al Qaeda and the Taliban's annual "fighting season." Mike mailed his first letter home to his parents in Staten Island on June 23, 2010:

> Hey Mom and Dad,
> I just talked to you guys on the phone. I couldn't say much about what I'm doing so I'll explain it here.
>   I flew into Kandahar Air Field a couple of weeks ago. Then I got moved to Forward Operating Base Lindsey. The FOB is only a ten-minute drive from the Air Field. The

reason I got moved is because I got tasked out to train up the Afghan soldiers. I'm going to be training them for three weeks and once I'm done, I will either fly out or convoy to FOB Howz-e Madad. That's where I'll be going out on patrols and other Army stuff.

I'm not going to lie to you when I say it's not the safest area. They say there's a lot of Taliban there so I'll do my best to write and call if I can.

Today, we met the Afghan soldiers for the first time. Their ages range from about 17 to some in their forties. Some know very little English. The Army gave us a translator but he speaks Pashto and the Afghan soldiers speak Dari, LOL. So basically, this is not going to be an easy three weeks.

They had me training some of the machine gunners on their weapons today. I showed them different firing positions and then we had a competition. I had them take apart their weapons and put them back together in two minutes. A lot of them did it—it was funny.

We will be working half-days because they complain that it gets too hot to train, which is stupid because they're going to be going out on patrols with us. Once we get to Howz-e Madad, we get Thursday and Friday off, too. So basically I'm going to be kind of bored.

I'm still talking to Courtney. She's doing well and I think she's going to be starting her rotations soon. She also just went to her friend's wedding and was one of the bridesmaids.

Well, I've got to go, I have a meeting at 2100 [9 p.m. local time]. I miss you guys and my truck, not gonna lie! Love you guys.

Love,
Mike

Courtney was the new lady in Mike's life. They met while Mike was stationed at Fort Campbell in Kentucky and she was finishing up medical school in neighboring Tennessee. They first struck up a conversation at a busy bar in downtown Nashville, exchanged phone numbers, and subsequently started visiting each other when their work and school schedules allowed.

Almost immediately, Mike knew Courtney was another one of those "great women" in his life. She had beautiful blond hair and eyes as bright as the intellect of an aspiring physician. In Mike, Courtney saw not just a brave American soldier but a funny, compassionate guy who loved life, his family, and friends. The glass was always half full for Mike, even on the eve of deploying to a desolate, desperate place like Kandahar.

"I'll be back before you know it," Mike told Courtney during one of their last phone calls before he deployed to Afghanistan from Fort Polk.

Courtney's first letter, which she had written on an online military platform called Hooah Mail for hand delivery to FOB Lindsey, was mailed on June 27, 2010. While it took a while for her message to reach the base, Mike excitedly tore open the stubs on the letter, which was typed out on US Army stationery:

Hey Babe!

What's up? So I miss you a lot, even more so today for some reason. You probably popped into my mind like 20 times today.

Wow, a glass of wine really makes me want to see you. :) You know what I miss right now? Your laugh. Your cute laugh though—you have a few different laughs and smiles and I miss the real cute one that you do when we're just being playful. Like when I say you're in a lot of trouble and then you laugh right before you kiss me! Alright, I'll stop being ridiculous.

I hope you're doing well. I think about what you're doing all the time. If you're too hot, too cold, hungry or not, think of me realizing how incredibly brave and amazing you are.

Okay, seriously I'm going to stop now. I'll talk to you soon! Goodnight babe—sweet dreams and I cannot wait to see you. Miss you!

XOXOXO
Court

Kandahar was indeed hot—in every sense of the word. The average temperature in June was 102 degrees and an astonishing 104 in July. Taliban and al Qaeda fighters seemed to be everywhere and were also making a concerted effort to penetrate the ranks of the Afghan National Army (ANA), which Mike and his fellow soldiers were playing a big role in training. Over the course of Mike's deployment, the threat of so-called "insider attacks" by terrorists posing as Afghan soldiers would dramatically increase.

An April 1, 2010, *New Yorker* article by Steve Coll outlined the pivotal role Kandahar would play in President Obama's Afghanistan troop surge. Once again, Mike found himself on the central front of a historically consequential attempt to turn around an American war:

> Admiral Mike Mullen, the Chairman of the Joint Chiefs, describes Kandahar as being "in this time frame . . . as critical in Afghanistan as Baghdad was in Iraq in the surge, writ large." Something like half or more of the thirty thousand additional troops ordered to Afghanistan by President Obama will take part in the campaign. The basic idea is that if international forces can chase the Taliban out of their heartland and gradually replace the current racketeering-infected provincial government with one

that is recognized by Afghans as more inclusive and less corrupt, then momentum in the broader war may swing against the Taliban.

The in-theater commanders who briefed reporters travelling with Mullen this week said they did not expect a formal "D-Day" launch of military operations in Kandahar, such as occurred in Marjah earlier this year. The rough timeline for "clearing" operations, i.e., the taking of territory from Taliban control by force, is planned to roll out gradually from late spring until well into the fall. The campaign's achievements or lack of them will no doubt be a critical element of the review of Afghan strategy due in December. Most of the action will take place in a number of suburban districts of Kandahar where the Taliban are mainly in control. There will also be a rollout of joint US-Afghan neighborhood security stations in Kandahar City, where the Afghan government is notionally in control but Taliban influence is heavy and rising. The plan is attempt to reduce violence and civilian casualties by organizing a rolling series of sub-district shuras in the hope that local power brokers will "invite" international forces to enter and set up control, and will at the same time "invite" the Taliban to scoot.

As Coll's analysis makes clear, to say the situation in Kandahar was complicated in mid-2010 would have been a severe understatement. From his experience in Iraq, Mike knew that the best way to handle the confusion was to focus on his mission and keep the soldiers in his company safe. Everything else was just background noise.

Brian Constantino was also deployed to Kandahar, but serving in a different company. Even though Tino and Mike would see each other almost every day, it wasn't quite the same in the beginning as

Iraq, as Mike noted in a letter to his parents: "I'm here with other guys in my unit but I don't know them," he wrote.

It didn't take long for Mike to start building a rapport with the fellow "Renegade" soldiers in his new company. Mike also built a reputation as being a tough but fair team leader. Those serving under him—particularly a soldier named Roy Patterson—became so endeared to Mike that they began emulating his every move. When Mike started wearing bandanas under his army helmet, so did many of the other guys, including Roy.

What the younger soldiers loved most about Mike was that even though he was occasionally strict, he was usually in the mood to joke around, regardless of rank. One particular incident that involved Mike being attacked by a dog wound up becoming a running joke inside their company.

Mike was repeatedly yelling "STOP!" at the animal until realizing the dog didn't know any English commands. As they went out on patrols in the ensuing months, Roy and the other guys would often imitate Mike yelling "STOP!" when they encountered a dog. While Mike would pretend to get mad about being made fun of by lower-ranking soldiers, he also found the incident funny and would usually laugh right along with them.

While Mike tried to zero in on training the Afghans at FOB Lindsey, the frequent explosions and bursts of gunfire he would hear outside the base highlighted the reality that working with foreign soldiers wouldn't be his only mission. As soon as those three weeks of training were complete, Mike—a "Strike Force" fire team leader—would head to FOB Howz-e Madad. There, he would likely spend significant time outside the wire fighting the Taliban in the very place where the repressive regime was conceived about fifteen years earlier.

When Mike arrived, American FOBs were springing up all over Afghanistan, the Taliban's and al Qaeda's home turf. CBS News republished a report by Nick Turse on this key element of the

Afghanistan surge strategy on October 22, 2010. The parallels to Mike's Iraq deployment couldn't have been more obvious:

> Some go by names steeped in military tradition like Leatherneck and Geronimo. Many sound fake-tough, like Ramrod, Lightning, Cobra, and Wolverine.
>
> Some display a local flavor, like Orgun-E, Howz-e Madad, and Kunduz. All, however, have one thing in common: they are US and allied forward operating bases, also known as FOBs.
>
> They are part of a base-building surge that has left the countryside of Afghanistan dotted with military posts, themselves expanding all the time, despite the drawdown of forces promised by President Obama beginning in July 2011.

Mike sent another letter home to his parents on July 11, 2010, just as he was finishing up his mission to train the Afghans on FOB Lindsey:

> *Hey Mom and Dad,*
>
> *How is everything? Today we got Sunday off because the ANA is doing culture training. It's weird how they're learning about their own culture, LOL. I think they're just trying to get out of real training. They're very lazy.*
>
> *One day we had them out training on spotting IEDs and how to react to them. They were complaining that it was too hot to train, LOL. We were the ones wearing all our gear and they were complaining?*
>
> *Yesterday we went into their barracks and hung out with them. Some of the guys were teaching me how to say some words in Dari and I was teaching them some English. I can now say "weapon," "watch," "uniform" and "boots" in Dari.*

I'll try to learn to start saying sentences but it will be a while, LOL.

I went shooting on July 4th with the ANA and I made a friend. He gave me a bead bracelet so I gave him my cancer awareness band. I don't think he knows what it means but he wears it every day.

Tomorrow we're going to teach them how to clear rooms like a SWAT team, so we'll see how it goes. Well, tell everyone I said hello. I miss you guys! I'll be done with training either on the 20th or the end of the month, then we convoy to FOB Howz-e Madad. Then, I'll start doing patrols.

> *Love,*
> *Mike*

While it took a little longer than expected, Mike completed his ANA training mission in early August and then made a perilous trek through the Taliban-infested terrain to reach his new FOB. He wrote home about the harrowing experience on August 11, 2010:

Hey Mom and Dad,
I made it down to Howz-e Madad okay! The convoy sucked! We had a truck break down on the way to the FOB. The truck that had to tow the broke down truck had to drive 15 mph because the tow bar would have broken if it went over that speed. Then we got stuck in traffic near a bridge—luckily we didn't get hit on the way down there.

So I stayed down there for a week, then my squad and I got pushed down to our patrol base. The living conditions aren't too bad. The patrol base (PB) is manned by a platoon of ANA soldiers and a platoon of US soldiers. We live in a tent with about 30 dudes. If we want to take a shower, we need to take a bucket, go to the water well, fill it up and then bring it to the shower. Then you fill the tank up that's connected to the shower head then take a shower.

We eat MREs for breakfast and lunch. For dinner, we BBQ on a grill. We even have a pet dog that's a stray that we named Dushka, which is an old Soviet machine gun (DShK). We have a weird sense of humor, LOL. The dog kind of looks like Sydney, except instead of brown and white it's brown and black. But she eats like her.

Today, we went out on a patrol to the village that's right near the PB and the dog came with us, LOL. The village was like a village in Iraq. There were mud huts and kids running around. One kid took out a cart with wheels and put jars of candy on it and started selling candy. I bought some from him—I gave him a dollar. We also gave the village a carpet for their mosque. Then, the high-ranking guys talked to the village elder who runs the village. Then, we walked back.

We got back and cooked some steaks and now we're about to go on guard. I'll be on ECP guard—ECP stands for entrance control point. It's the point where you go in and out from. We've got a truck blocking the entrance and at night, we take this truck with a computer that controls the weapons system on the truck and you sit in the back and look at a computer screen. It's like a video camera and you control the weapon with a joystick. The camera on the 50 cal [caliber machine gun] has a day/night sight. It's pretty high-speed shit, LOL.

Anyway, I hope things went well with Kelly—I can't wait to find out if she had a boy or a girl. Tell the family I said hello. I miss you guys and I'll call when I can.

Love,
Mike

Mike was later thrilled to learn that Kelly and Dave had welcomed a baby girl, Ava, the day before he wrote his letter. Ava was Mike's first and only niece, and he couldn't wait to meet her.

Early on, Mike realized that his second deployment would be far more intense than his first in terms of combat, which was logical since he was serving as a fire team leader operating out of one of southern Afghanistan's most crucial American bases. FOB Howz-e Madad had been in the Taliban's crosshairs ever since construction began on the now-sprawling base. Almost every day that summer, the enemy would do something to test the FOB's security, whether through surveillance or actual attacks.

In a summer 2010 edition of *The Heartbeat,* an official magazine of the 101st Airborne Division's 2nd Brigade Combat Team, US Army public affairs officers explained why FOB Howz-e Madad was so critical not just to the mission in Kandahar but to the overall war in Afghanistan: "Located in the western part of (Zhari) District, right off of Afghanistan's famous Highway 1, is the base responsible for every 'Strike Force' mission," the army's article said. "Forward Operating Base Howz-e Madad has been the center of coordination since 'Strike Force' began expanding its borders earlier this summer."

The article outlined how Mike's FOB was used to plan joint missions with ANA soldiers and transport troops to and from various southern Afghanistan bases via helicopter. Those warfighters included the soldiers in Mike's Bravo Company, who would often shuttle to and from nearby PBs scattered throughout the Arghandab River valley. The FOB's medical clinic was also essential in treating wounded soldiers before they were flown to nearby Kandahar Airfield, where there was a much bigger hospital.

The piece also explained what life was like on the FOB for deployed soldiers like Mike:

Located near the HEM [Howz-e Madad] chapel is one of the more advanced Morale Welfare and Recreation Centers in the Combined Task Force Strike area. With its 40 computers and 20 phones, HEM's MWR Center allows soldiers to connect to friends and family.

"When soldiers are out on missions for extended lengths of time, it's important for them to have a place to come where they relax and talk with their loved ones," said SGT James Boldizsar, Strike Force chaplain assistant and a major contributor in the setting up of the FOB's MWR. "Whether it's checking their Facebook page, using the phones to call the States or just sitting down and watching a movie on the big screen TV, our soldiers come here to unwind for a little bit."

FOB Howz-e Madad houses one of the most historical units in the 101st Airborne Division and what's inside its borders is crucial to the success of the FOB's surrounding areas.

"We are here to really make a change," said [Sergeant First Class Gerald] Napper. "The soldiers of 2nd Battalion are located where they are for a reason. They have been chosen by command, along with ANA counterparts, to lead the charge in securing an important part of the Zhari District."

FOB Howz-e Madad, which was essentially a dust bowl lined with endless rows of huge tents, was in a valley close to a town center and major trade area, which was reachable via Afghanistan's Highway 1. Mike's company was in between the valley and the Taliban's birthplace, which was just to the south. To their north was what had essentially become a refugee zone for locals to escape the fighting.

In every conceivable way, Mike was right smack in the middle of everything, which was underscored by the almost daily Taliban attacks on his base's guard tower. Within a few weeks, waking up to the sounds of gunfire had become routine.

Mike once again wrote home to his parents on August 24, 2010:

Hey Mom and Dad,

How are you guys? I'm down at my PB for five days. We had a crazy day a couple of days ago. I finally got into a firefight.

There was a PB that was under attack, so we got called out to help out. There, we took fire from the wood line south of the base. We couldn't see them, but they kept shooting at us and the birds [helicopters], so we were shooting back into the wood line. I shot about half of my magazine and M203 rounds. I am pretty lethal with the grenade launcher, LOL.

My squad leader would shoot tracers to where we thought the contact was coming from and I would put 203 rounds right where he was shooting. One of my rounds accidentally hit a mud hut but nothing happened. I couldn't believe it. The mud hut took the hit like a champ!

It was one hell of a fireworks show. We had Kiowas and Apache attack helicopters come down doing their gun runs, then pulling out and coming back. They were shooting their machine guns, rockets and Hellfire missiles.

Getting shot at was crazy, though. I could hear the rounds crack near me. We stood up on a wall shooting and mostly watching the birds. We stood there for about three hours. It was an awesome day and none of us got hurt.

Today, our patrol got cancelled. The air status was black so the birds couldn't fly. So, I had guard duty to pull and then I did my laundry in a bucket next to the water well. And we just found out that we're short on water and we don't know when we can get resupplied. So now we can't go on patrols or even work out, LOL. The higher-ups messed up the water count.

I hope to hear from you guys soon. Let me know when you get my letters. Tell everyone I said hello and I miss you guys!

Love,
Mike

Getting shot at by the Taliban for hours on end while rationing water wouldn't seem "awesome" to most people, but for Mike it was a dream come true. This was what he wanted to be doing, not driving a commanding officer around Iraq while never really getting into the action with his friends and fellow soldiers. Even though conditions were hot and the pressure from the enemy was heavy, Mike mostly had a smile on his face during the early part of that deployment. His smile got even bigger when more letters arrived from Courtney:

Dear Michael—I just FREAKED out because I almost couldn't find your new address on this thing! But don't you worry, I took a deep breath and tried again.

On a lighter note, I want to hear about what you are doing . . . I'm starting to forget your smiles and just the way that your face moves when you talk. :(I have the picture but you just have a smile that you have to see in person to really appreciate. I can't wait to see you. If you could stop popping into my head every five minutes that would be great, LOL. Miss your face!
Courtney

Over the next few weeks, Mike's company continued moving between the FOB and the valley. Tino's was tasked with holding a hill overlooking the area where his close friend was running and gunning to and from various PBs. The front formed by the Strike Force companies was more like an arc than a straight line through the valley, as Mike's commanding officers wanted the Taliban to feel like they were surrounded by heavily armed and superior-trained American forces.

Even though their companies were still split apart, Mike and Tino began to pass each other more frequently as activity—and the number of firefights—increased. Most of the time, it would be because Mike fired so many rocket-propelled grenades (RPGs) at enemy positions that he would frequently have to head back up to the FOB to replenish his supply.

"I'm sick of always having to go back and get more grenades!" Mike would often joke as he passed through Tino's position.

While some soldiers mocked the Taliban and their primitive ways, the enemy fighting the Americans in Kandahar during the surge were mostly well trained and well placed. They had home-field advantage and had spent the previous nine years learning how to utilize it. For the most part, the enemy that Mike and Tino were fighting had plenty of support, money, and supplies to make the Americans work—and bleed—for every inch of territory gained in the valley that summer. Being that he and his fellow "Renegades" were on the ground level instead of up on a hill like Tino's company, Mike was almost always in danger.

Many soldiers would try to shield their moms and dads from the realities of war, but Mike felt he owed it to his to be honest. From the beginning, Mike had always wanted his parents to know where he was and what he was doing. It was thus impossible for Linda and Bob to read the letter he wrote on September 3, 2010, without worrying whether their son would make it home alive from his second combat deployment:

Mom and Dad,

Hey guys, just want to say Happy Anniversary! Thank you for the pictures of [Kelly's] baby. I was happy to see her.

I'm doing alright here, just been having some really close calls. I've been lucky so far; this place is not like Iraq at all. Rumor has it they might make this a nine-month deployment but that's just a rumor for now. I'm still going home [on leave] in January. I'm counting down the days, LOL. I've got a long time to go.

I've been bounding to different patrol bases here and there. It makes time go by fast, but it's always a pain to pack and unpack my gear. For the past two nights we slept on the ground near our trucks because the building they have in the PB didn't have any space for us. It wasn't bad sleeping under the stars. At night it cools down, so it's nice.

I hope you guys are doing well and Dad is enjoying his new truck. Please don't forget about mine, LOL! Tell everyone I said hello; I miss you guys and thank you for the package. Write some letters when you have time.

Love,

Mike

It's impossible to know exactly what Mike was thinking while he lay under the stars, but one would guess he spent some time missing his family, his friends, and Courtney. Would he ever get to see them again? If he did, would he be missing an arm or leg or be in the same state of mind he had been when he last saw them? If he was blown up or shot during the deployment, what would he do for a living after the army? The emotions of a long combat tour were not new for Mike, but the frequency and intensity of the risks he was facing were weighing on him more than ever.

A series of incidents during the ensuing weeks would throw everything Mike thought he knew about being an American soldier into question. Even spending fifteen straight months in Iraq couldn't have prepared him for the unprecedented challenges he would soon face. As Mike was about to learn the hard way, "war is hell" isn't a cliché but a harsh reality—in his case, of a dreadful valley that would leave permanent marks on his soul.

CHAPTER 8

EVERY SECOND COUNTS

September 5, 2010, was supposed to be a day like any other. Mike would start out keeping watch atop his PB's guard tower before going out on foot for a patrol mission in the afternoon.

Mike was doing his guard duty and scanning the valley for threats when he heard an unmistakable *BOOM*. It was the sound of a massive enemy IED detonating almost exactly where another American patrol was headed that morning.

As Mike raised his weapon and got on the radio to report the explosion, his heart sank and he became nauseated. As he could see through his binoculars, a giant plume of smoke was rising from a large mine-resistant ambush-protected (MRAP) vehicle that had flipped over near a hill that was about a thousand yards from Mike's compound. One of the passengers in the massive, mangled military truck—to Mike's horror—was Brian Constantino.

Tino had actually just stopped by to see Mike during a supply run he made right before the mission. They hung out and joked around for a few minutes until Tino and his fellow soldiers had to head back outside the wire. It made Mike even more sick to his stomach to think that might have been the last time he saw his close friend alive.

Mike began to panic as his fellow soldiers scrambled to convoy out to the blast site and help the wounded. As fate would have it, Mike wasn't able to join them since he happened to be on guard duty that day. Even though his best army friend's life was in danger—or perhaps already over—Mike could not abandon his post. He had no choice but to rely on the men in his company to hopefully pull his buddy safely out of the burning vehicle.

Tino was trapped. The five-hundred-pound IED had torpedoed the giant MRAP—which was designed specifically to fend off IEDs and land mines—into an almost impossible position. The vehicle's rear was in the sand with its heavily damaged hood pointed straight up toward the sky. Tino's driver had broken most of his bones and the vehicle's gunner was also badly hurt.

As for Tino himself, the blast had broken his right foot and nearly taken his left foot off completely. He had a broken back and severely ruptured tendons in one of his shoulders. Thankfully, he was alive—thanks in large part to Mike calling in helicopters from the guard tower and soldiers from Bravo and other Strike Force companies coming to pull Tino and his injured battle buddies out of the smoldering vehicle.

Mike barely had a chance to say goodbye at the PB's clinic before Tino was flown out of the valley that night to receive better medical care. Watching the helicopter ascend out of his small sandy base while carrying his friend was the loneliest feeling Mike had ever felt as an American soldier. He was relieved that Tino had survived, but simultaneously dreading the next few months in Afghanistan without him.

An anguished Mike wrote home about his friend's injury on September 10, 2010:

Mom and Dad,
My buddy Brian from Germany got hurt. He got banged
up pretty bad and got sent back to Germany. His truck got

blown up by an IED. It put the truck on its backside and the nose of the truck was facing straight up. The guys in his platoon said he messed up his legs and back. He won't be coming back here at all.

I miss him already—I would bump into him when we would refit at FOB Howz-e Madad. We would sit and talk about our crazy days in Europe and about life. He was the closest friend I had here.

I'm at FOB Terminator. We're about to do a big mission and we're supporting the Special Forces [SF]. We will be flying in Shithooks [a derogatory nickname often used by soldiers for old CH-47 Chinook helicopters] landing outside the village and we will be providing supporting fire for the SF when they go through the village and get rid of the terrorist cell block.

Once they do that, we will push through and hold down the village and set up a PB. They said it should be a seventy-two-hour mission, but we will see. We will be living out of our rucks [backpacks] and carrying our rucks with us as well.

Well, take care and I'll call when I can.

Love,

Mike

The relationship between soldiers is unique. In the case of Mike and Tino, they had spent every day for the past three years going through training, two combat deployments, and memorable vacations together. To suddenly not have Tino by his side (or at least nearby, as was the case in Afghanistan) would prove to be one of Mike's greatest challenges as a deployed warfighter. On top of his friend's absence was the fact that conditions on the ground in southern Afghanistan seemed to be getting more perilous by the hour.

Just ten days after Tino and his teammates were nearly killed, the US and NATO launched Operation Dragon Strike. The wide-ranging mission had the lofty objective of finally crushing the Taliban in Kandahar Province. The goal was not just killing enemy fighters and seizing territory, but working with the local population to hold those gains after a given battle subsided. Mike and the men of Bravo Company would play a huge role in the historic effort, which would last until the end of the year and ultimately draw in not just al Qaeda, but members of Iran's Quds Force, which had long been accused of terrorist activity by the US government.

Before Tino's injury, the pair and others had joked that Mike always seemed to be the first one to get shot at on a given mission. It was the same thing at most bars they went to: there was usually someone there who wanted to fight Mike because they were jealous of his confident attitude, New York accent, or popularity with the girls. For whatever reason, the enemy similarly seemed to love shooting at Mike in Afghanistan—until he broke out his grenade launcher, that is.

The foot patrols Mike went on were usually through thick fields of grapes, marijuana, and poppies that lined Highway 1. Giant ditches full of water and fertilizer lined each field, which meant that when a firefight began, the first move was usually to jump into the closest ditch. Given that some of the trees in the grape rows would grow upward of eight feet tall and a soldier's boots would often be stuck in the mud, combat was even more challenging. Fighting conditions in those miserable ditches actually resembled World War I's infamous trench warfare much more than anything Mike had encountered in Iraq.

Even as the weather began to cool that fall, heat was almost always a factor, which therefore made the firefights even more difficult. Mike would not only have to worry about running out of grenades during a long battle, but water. Lugging a belt of 20–25 grenades in addition to weapons and a ruck full of tools would often get extremely taxing while trudging through Kandahar's seemingly never-ending grapevine trenches.

During enemy encounters, Mike often found himself launching all of his grenades, which meant a given firefight was heavy and sustained. He would usually fire his M203, shoot some more, then jump over grape rows, then start firing all over again. Mike was in excellent physical condition, but even the toughest, most seasoned soldier would have found that battle routine tough to sustain over a period of several months.

The only thing keeping Mike going was getting home to see his family, his friends, Courtney, and most of all Tino, who was receiving treatment in Germany before being flown back to a military hospital in the United States.

"Keep your head up, Ollie," Tino would often tell Mike during their frequent phone calls and Facebook message exchanges. "If I made it out of there without getting killed, so can you!"

Mike also continued to hear from Courtney.

"No matter what our relationship is, thanks for being you and making me more of me," Courtney wrote in a card she mailed to Mike's FOB. "I'll always be here for you—whatever and no matter what it is. I miss you the most."

Mike sent Courtney a lengthy Facebook message during a particularly stressful chapter of his first Afghanistan deployment. Like countless deployed soldiers, sailors, airmen, and Marines, Mike was trying to balance life during wartime with trying to stay in touch and maintain relationships with the people he cared about most:

> I always wanted to be a soldier and now that I am, it's a
> tiring job and it's tough handling work and my personal
> life. Courtney, I just want to let you know that I really care
> about you and I support you in anything that you do. I'm

*sorry I kind of questioned us for a second, I just know that
me being away is tough on you and I'm really sorry.*

*I'm also sorry for comparing you to other relationships
I had in the past. It's just hard for me to handle being over
here and starting a relationship. Also, the night when we
were in Philadelphia and you told me you loved me, I froze
up inside and I got nervous. What popped into my head
was me leaving to come over here and just thinking about
what if something happened to me. I just don't want to
hurt you like that.*

I miss you a lot and can't wait to hold you again!!!
Love,
Mike

The last known letter that Mike mailed home to his parents
during that difficult deployment was written on October 12,
2010, a little less than a month since the launch of Operation
Dragon Strike. It contained a huge revelation about Strike Force's
ongoing efforts to bring the terrorists who nearly killed Tino and
his teammates to justice:

Dear Mom and Dad,
*Life over here is busy. We've been doing our big push south
trying to find the Taliban and get them out of here so the
people can come back to their homes again. The Taliban
forces families out of their houses and used their homes as
safehouses and also fighting positions.*

*Our first night, we air assaulted into a farm field from
a CH-47 "shithook" as dad calls it, LOL. Then in the
morning, we went into one compound and arrested eleven
IED makers and placers. They were all brothers working
for the Taliban. We're pretty sure those were the guys who
planted the IED that Brian drove over.*

The day after that, we got into a firefight, which was awesome because I got to shoot a smoke grenade with my M203 to mark the enemy's position so the birds could fly in and shoot shit up. And they came in hot! They were shooting 50 cals and rockets. Then, we took fire from another area and I marked it with another smoke grenade, and the birds came right back shooting shit up. It was awesome.

After the shooting stopped, we continued clearing compounds that the Taliban were using when we came across fighting positions, small tunnels and IED-making materials. Once we were done, we found an empty walled-off compound and we set up camp. There are two small mud houses, so we either sleep in there or outside.

Living conditions suck. It's hot during the day and cold at night. We also go out during the night to see if the Taliban are putting IEDs along the road. My squad went out, I took point and my M-14 gunner saw a guy through his thermals, which pick up heat. The guy was hiding behind some bushes across a dried up wadi [ravine] so I got my guys into position and told my squad leader what was going on. I got the okay to go ahead with my plan so I pushed up closer to where this guy was with my M-14 gunner and I shot a parachute flare to light up the sky.

The guy took off running with a weapon. My M-14 gunner shot at him and missed. I tried shooting my M203 at him but I missed also. It was an intense night but we scared him off and hopefully kept him from putting in IEDs.

So after five days of being out here, we came back to the FOB to refit for 24 hours and then we pushed back. We got back to our compound, took over force protection and guarded the compound while the other squads went out on patrol. So, we have this man come up to the compound *waving his hands while dressed like a regular Afghan and he's saying he's an American, LOL.*

At first, we tell him to go away and then he starts getting shot at and he's yelling at us saying "why are you shooting at me?" And we're like, "this guy's speaking perfect English." So we're like, "we're not shooting at you, come to us" and he runs into the compound. I stopped him and searched him. He's a 6'4" or 6'5" Black guy who's a photographer that got captured by the Taliban in Kandahar City. He works for the AP [Associated Press] and had been missing for three or four months.

He managed to escaped on foot early in the morning and had been running away for three hours straight. We were like "what the HELL"—we didn't know what to think. We kept questioning him, gave him water and he told us his story about how he was in Kandahar City and met a teenage boy who spoke English. He went into a shop to buy clothes and the teenage boy went over to some Taliban and "sold" him. The Taliban walked into the shop and put a grenade to his chest and said "come with us, you have been sold."

So, they took him away and questioned him. They thought he was some kind of soldier and at first, they didn't believe him. But after a while they realized that he was telling the truth. They didn't beat him up, just chained him up for a couple of days. They even let him write a letter and one of the Taliban emailed the letter to his parents. They even let him call home once.

They moved him around at night—then one night one of the guards that was watching his room got up and went to have tea with the other guys and that's when he made a break for it. Crazy story, huh? It was like something out of a movie.

Anyway, I got a letter from Courtney and she's told
me they're getting rid of Hooah Mail or they're making
people pay for it, which is bullshit! Sorry for the language
but that's just messed up. A lot of my buddies' wives use
that too. If you guys could make a complaint that would be
awesome. Anyway, I miss you guys and I hope to hear from
you soon.

Love always,
Mike

Mike also enclosed a letter for his parents to give to his sister Kelly, since his address book was packed away at another base. His company always seemed to be convoying between PBs, COPs, and FOBs throughout the Zhari district of Kandahar Province, which made it difficult to keep track of his possessions.

During Operation Dragon Strike, Mike conducted approximately five air-assault raids on enemy positions and personally led his fire team through and out of countless firefights. He would earn multiple awards during the twelve-month deployment, including an Army Commendation Medal, Afghanistan Campaign Ribbon with one campaign star, Overseas Ribbon, NATO ISAF (International Security Assistance Force) ribbon, Valorous Unit Citation, and Presidential Unit Citation.

The awards meant nothing to Mike compared to the events of December 12, 2010, which he would carry with him for the rest of his life.

Mike and his company were in the small village of Sangsar, which was just north of the Arghandab River. The soldiers were there to work "shoulder to shoulder" (as was the US Army's official motto in Afghanistan) with ANA forces at what had become one of their strongholds. While it was technically an Afghan base, there was always at least one platoon of American soldiers living there to train and integrate with their ANA counterparts. They were also helping with construction, as some sections of the compound were not yet finished.

It was about 9:00 a.m. local time when Mike and his fellow soldiers were shaken by a powerful, earthshaking explosion. Within seconds, a massive plume of smoke blanketed the entire valley as sheer panic ensued. On a much smaller scale, the sights and sounds Mike was subjected to over the next several hours were similar to what firefighters, police officers, and first responders experienced on 9/11.

As Mike and his fellow soldiers would later discover, a vehicle-mounted IED was driven up a short road resembling a driveway. The van's driver ignored a group of ANA soldiers who told him to stop and pulled right up to the side of the base. To everyone's horror, between five hundred and one thousand pounds of explosives packed inside the van then blasted directly into the wall of a building where dozens of American soldiers were sleeping. They lay defenseless as the explosion blasted through the solid mud wall and caused the ceiling to collapse.

Like many buildings in Afghanistan, this one was probably over a thousand years old, which meant the "moon sand" it was originally built out of had been hardening in the sun for centuries. When the roof collapsed, the sleeping soldiers were hit not just by crumbling sand but by what looked and probably felt like heavy chunks of falling concrete. The soldiers who were not killed by the initial blast were now buried beneath a huge pile of rubble and at risk of suffocation if rescuers didn't reach them soon.

This was the moment when all of Mike's many years of training immediately and instinctively kicked in. Before he mounted a rescue mission, Mike knew that he and his men had to first secure the compound. If there were still enemy fighters running inside the perimeter, they had to be neutralized in order to ensure there were enough Americans left on the compound to save their trapped fellow soldiers.

"Weapons, check! Body armor, check!" Mike and his Strike Force teammates yelled back and forth as they ran into the dusty darkness that had covered their compound. The air was so thick they could barely breathe and the fires created by the IED were hotter than anything they had felt thus far in southern Afghanistan, which was saying something.

Mike heard no secondary gunfire or explosions, which was good news. Instead, though, he heard the screams and coughs of his barricaded brothers-in-arms, which was dreadful.

After circling around the devastated compound with their weapons, Mike concluded it was secure and assigned several soldiers to set up a temporary perimeter to ensure that no more Taliban or al Qaeda fighters could penetrate the base until American and Afghan reinforcements arrived. In an environment where the enemy thrived on secondary attacks, Mike's training and experience had drilled into his mind that security always had to come first. Now that the compound was relatively safe, all of his attention could turn to rescuing the trapped soldiers. There was no time to spare.

What Mike saw upon arriving at the remnants of the building truly did resemble a burning stack of World Trade Center rubble—much like the digital picture he had drawn as a boy. He briefly lowered his head upon realizing that under those heavy blocks of mud were the remains of several fallen friends.

After allowing himself to be briefly overcome by emotion, Mike shook his head, cleared the cobwebs, and fully focused on saving anyone who was still alive. The time had come to pour every single ounce of his energy into lifting his fellow soldiers out of suffocation and almost certain death. It was then that Mike decided to rally his fellow troops on the rescue and recovery effort.

"LET'S FUCKING GO!" he screamed with a vigor few around him had ever heard. It helped create a sense of urgency that set the tone for what would be an emotional and frantic mission.

Every pound of iron Mike had pumped while working out during and between deployments helped him lift up those mud blocks at an almost superhuman level and pace. His fellow soldiers were also working hard, but nevertheless struggling to keep up. Everyone was sweating, coughing, and occasionally crying when the body of someone they knew was found beneath the rubble. It was a harrowing and horrific scene that would have brought even the most hardened American warrior to his or her knees.

"THERE!" Mike yelled while pointing to a section of rubble. "I see a foot!"

To make matters worse for those trapped under the collapsed ceiling, they were not in uniform when the powerful explosion hit. The soldiers were mostly in pajamas while wearing socks or nothing at all on their feet. As a result, the injuries sustained by those lucky enough to make it out of the pile were even more substantial than they would have been with footwear.

As Mike pointed out more arms and legs beneath the rubble and he and his fellow soldiers knelt on top of piles to claw, push, and pull, there were terrified soldiers staggering through the huge pile wearing only sleep clothes. Some of the shaken survivors still couldn't fully comprehend what had happened while they were fast asleep. It was a surreal and terrifying experience for everyone who was there.

The eleven surviving soldiers who wound up being pulled out of the collapsed mud hut on that terrible day would never forget the faces of their valiant rescuers, including Mike. The faces everyone would remember most, however, belonged to the six American heroes who lost their lives during the brutal terrorist attack. The fallen 101st Airborne heroes came from across the country they volunteered to serve and from a wide range of backgrounds and beliefs. Tragically, none of the young men had the opportunity to live beyond the age of twenty-five:

Corporal Sean M. Collins, 25, Ewa Beach, Hawaii

Corporal Willie A. McLawhorn Jr., 23, Conway, North Carolina

Specialist Patrick D. Deans, 22, Orlando, Florida

Specialist Kenneth E. Necochea Jr., 21, San Diego, California

Specialist Derek T. Simonetta, 21, Redwood City, California

Specialist Jorge E. Villacis, 24, Sunrise, Florida

While attending the ensuing memorial services and mourning the dead, a terrible sound began echoing inside Mike's ears. It was the sound of trapped soldiers gasping for air—their mouths filled with mud and sand and their minds filled with confusion and panic. Pulling out bodies—living and dead—had already started taking a huge toll on Mike and several other soldiers who were on the ground that day.

"The soldiers at the combat outpost are 'working through' their grief," said a US Army article quoting Major General John F. Campbell published six days after the attack. "They're not going to let this stand between them and getting the mission done.

"The soldiers went right back out and did some operations to attack what they thought potentially were the guys that worked to plan this [attack]," the general added.

The Taliban had already claimed responsibility for the murders, with spokesman Qari Yousuf Ahmadi subsequently telling *The New York Times* that "we will carry out similar attacks in the future."

Nearly five hundred US service members were killed in Afghanistan in 2010, which was by far the deadliest year of what would wind up being America's longest war. Mike knew several, including the six heroes killed on December 12 and many more who nearly lost their lives. When they returned from southern Afghanistan to Fort Campbell, Mike's best army friend, Brian Constantino, who had spent the last five months in the hospital, would be waiting in a wheelchair to greet Mike and his battle buddies.

When Mike woke up at night to those horrible sounds of suffocating soldiers that he couldn't get out of his head, he would often make himself a promise. If Mike ever again found himself in a similar situation, he would react and respond at an even faster pace. During war's unrelenting and unpredictable chaos, as Sergeant Michael Harold Ollis had learned over the course of two combat deployments, every second counts.

CHAPTER 9

THE BIG LEAGUES

Mike returned from Afghanistan to Kentucky in the summer of 2011. After a few weeks of rest and recuperation, he resumed a demanding army training regimen. Mike consistently scored an incredible three hundred out of three hundred on his physical training tests, which commanded the respect of his instructors, superior officers, and fellow 101st Airborne Division paratroopers.

With two deployments under his belt plus having accumulated his Air Assault wings and many medals, it would have been difficult to find a more accomplished twenty-two-year-old infantry soldier in the United States Army. As had been the case since he was a teenager in JROTC, though, Mike believed he could reach even greater heights as both a soldier and a leader.

In September 2011, Mike received a noncommissioned officer (NCO) evaluation from the US Army. In the report, his squad leader, platoon leader, and company commander heaped universal praise on Mike's tireless efforts during his yearlong deployment to Afghanistan.

"Totally dedicated to [his] unit, mission and soldiers; a true credit to the NCO Corp," the first of three bulleted comments read. "Exhibited the highest standards of discipline, loyalty and integrity for soldiers to follow."

"Unfailingly displayed the example for all soldiers to emulate," the final comment said.

Citing Mike's "tactically sound judgment" during "40 direct fire engagements with insurgents," his commanders said that the soldier had "demonstrated excellent stamina and mental fortitude during continuous combat operations in arduous climate and terrain." They also noted that Mike had "successfully led [his] fire team in over 250 combat patrols and seven BN [battalion] level Air Assault operations in Zhari and Maiwand districts, Kandahar Province, Afghanistan."

Mike's actions had saved lives, from the harrowing roof-collapse rescue operation to "allowing the platoon to find and destroy over 12 dismounted IEDs." As a result, his commanders raved about his "outstanding performance from a quality NCO" and concluded that the soldier was "undoubtedly capable of [an] assignment of greater responsibility."

At the end of the 2011 report, Mike learned that he hadn't just achieved his dream of becoming a sergeant in the US Army. He had exceeded his own expectations.

"Promote to Staff Sergeant now" was his company commander's overall recommendation. For the third time in just over three years, Mike had earned a higher rank. While he would have to wait a few more months for the promotion paperwork to be processed, the good news arrived just in time for his twenty-third birthday.

With his pending promotion came new orders. Soon-to-be staff sergeant Ollis was reassigned to the Second Battalion, Twenty-Second Infantry Regiment, First Brigade Combat Team of the US Army's Tenth Mountain Division. He would be stationed at Fort Drum in his home state of New York, which meant that Mike would only be about three hundred miles from his family, which had another new member. Mike's third nephew, Thomas, had been welcomed by Kim and Bill on January 15, 2011, while his brave uncle was still busy squaring off with the Taliban in Afghanistan.

Being reassigned to Fort Drum meant that Mike was even closer to Courtney, who was continuing her medical studies in nearby Rochester, New York. Having broken up and got back together a few times, Mike and Courtney weren't sure exactly where their relationship was going. Instead of spending that fall and winter trying to plan out their future, however, the couple decided to make the most of their time together.

While nothing had been officially announced, Mike strongly suspected that another Afghanistan deployment was somewhere on the horizon. That meant that whenever possible, he would jump in the car with Courtney and head home to see family and friends. They liked taking the Staten Island Ferry to Manhattan, where the couple enjoyed seeing Broadway shows and experiencing New York City nightlife. They also took a memorable trip to the Split Rock Resort in Pennsylvania's Pocono Mountains with Kim and Bill, as well as to Hershey Park with William, Joseph, and Thomas, who loved joining their uncle on what had been his favorite ride as a child, a truck-driving simulator called "Convoy." Mike loved spending time with his nephews and niece.

On December 31, 2011, Mike was thrilled to play host for New Year's Eve festivities in Times Square. Jason, who served with Mike in Iraq and was also on those crazy trips to Europe, came to New York with his wife, Amy. Mike approached the trip as he would a combat mission: meticulously planning out every detail to ensure his friends would have the best possible time. His knowledge of the New York City subway system was a little rusty thanks to spending several years away from home, which led to some gentle ribbing from his dad.

As the old Iraq War buddies drank some beers and caught up during the trip, Jason was initially surprised by how hard Mike was taking the previous Afghanistan deployment. Jason's perception of Mike's state of mind was not negative but, rather, he saw raw emotions from Mike that were absent the first few months after Iraq.

"We were getting blown up or shot at almost every day, Jason," Mike said. "It was freaking intense over there."

Knowing that he was probably heading back to Afghanistan was also weighing heavily on Mike.

"As you know, we almost lost Tino last time," Mike said. "I just can't let anything happen to my guys."

"Just remember that you can't control everything out there, Ollie," Jason said. "Try not to worry so much."

Jason was also surprised to learn that Mike was still deciding whether to reenlist during what would most likely be his third combat tour. He still had about eighteen months to make a final decision, but the fact that Mike was even thinking about life after the army was shocking to those who knew him best. Mike's entire existence had been about being a soldier, but the strains of that second deployment were beginning to change his outlook on life.

While Mike was still a guy who reveled in making other people laugh, those who knew him best noticed that he was smiling the slightest bit less after his most recent deployment. None of his friends understood the emotions Mike was feeling better than his old friend Bolivar, who—like Mike—had already served combat deployments to Iraq and Afghanistan. Bolivar loved being a marine, but the scars of battle had resulted in increased anxiety, nightmares, and other symptoms of post-traumatic stress. He was particularly worried about his next deployment, which—again, like Mike—would be a return trip to Afghanistan.

While taking the Staten Island Ferry into the city one chilly 2012 Saturday night to hit the bars with their group of friends, Bolivar decided to confide in his close friend and fellow Iraq and Afghanistan veteran.

"I'm worried this next tour is gonna fucking get me, Mike," he said. "I've already cheated death so many times. How are you doing with everything, bro?" he added.

"It's not about me, man," Mike said. "It's about my guys."

Bolivar always admired how Mike never seemed to worry about himself. While everyone who volunteers to serve their country is inherently brave, Mike was truly selfless in every sense of the word. He had an innate sense of ownership—everyone around Mike was *his* responsibility and his alone. Whether deployed or back home, Mike maintained a laser-like focus on the soldiers in his unit instead of himself. Bolivar had first noticed those qualities back in JROTC, where it was obvious that Mike was a natural-born leader who would excel in the military.

Even in less flattering moments when Mike, Bolivar, and their friends got in trouble together over the years, Mike would always step up and take the blame. One moment that stuck out for Bolivar was when Mike's mom caught them drinking while underage in the hot tub and was extremely upset, as any good mother would be. Without hesitation, Mike raised his hand and admitted to illegally buying all the beer. It wasn't exactly true, but Mike didn't want to see any of his friends get into trouble.

"I'm glad you're doing okay, Mike," Bolivar said as the massive orange ferry passed the lit-up Statue of Liberty and the future Freedom Tower, which was being built to replace the World Trade Center. "I've gotta be honest—I'm not. All that shit I saw over there is really messing with my head."

Mike then put his arm around his good friend's shoulders.

"It's okay to feel that way," he said. "I understand what you're going through, man—I really do. You can talk to me about this anytime."

"Thanks, Mike," Bolivar said.

That night on the Staten Island Ferry wound up being the one and only time Mike and Bolivar ever had a heart-to-heart about their jobs as American war fighters. Even though Bolivar continued to struggle with post-traumatic stress, Mike's words of encouragement would stay with the marine during his next combat deployment and beyond.

Mike didn't tell Bolivar that he was still trying to escape his own demons from Afghanistan. True to form, Mike wanted to focus on helping his friend without turning the spotlight on himself.

Time and time again, Mike's nightmares would conclude with him trying to pull a suffocating soldier from a pile of rubble after the roof collapsed. Mike had hoped that the gasps for air he kept hearing in his head would go away after a few months of being back home. If anything, though, they were only getting louder.

After his group of friends left a get-together in his parents' backyard one night in New Dorp, Mike sat down with his dad on their screened-in back porch. It was chilly and normally they would have gone inside, but Bob could tell his son had something important he wanted to talk about.

Once they sat down, Mike began to explain exactly what had happened in the village of Sangsar, Afghanistan, on December 12, 2010. It only took a few minutes before the soldier broke down and started to cry.

"The sand was coming out of their nostrils, Dad," Mike said while putting his head in his hands. "We got a bunch of guys out, but the others—I just couldn't help them. All I hear in my head is them trying to breathe."

Bob knew exactly how it felt to be haunted by a particular sight or sound from the battlefield. After all, he had struggled with similar memories from Vietnam for most of his life before finally learning how to cope.

"Michael, I love you and it kills me to see you like this," Bob said in a quiet tone of voice while putting his arm around his son, just like Mike had done to Bolivar. "But now I need you to listen to me, son: you cannot let yourself fixate on what happened that day."

"But what if I had gotten there sooner, Dad?" Mike interrupted. "What if we could have saved even one of those six guys?"

"You had to make sure the base was secure first, right?" said Bob, having been through similar scenarios in combat. "There was nothing else you could have done.

"Michael, I'll help you in any way I can, but you need to find a way to move forward," Bob continued. "What other choice do we have? What's done is done."

"Thanks, Dad," Mike said before giving his father a hug.

Staff Sergeant Michael Ollis and the brave men and women of the Bushmaster 2–22nd Infantry Regiment—Triple Deuce, as it was nicknamed—were set to deploy to the rugged mountains of eastern Afghanistan in early 2013. Before leaving, Mike had the privilege of meeting his fourth nephew, Matthew, who was welcomed to the world on September 10, 2012, while Mike was on predeployment leave.

Adding to the joy, Kelly and Dave asked Mike to be Matthew's godfather. He was thrilled to be able to attend his nephew's christening shortly before heading out for yet another training mission. Mike, his sisters, their husbands, and the kids were also able to attend a New York Jets football game together before he left.

Just over six weeks after Matthew was born, Mike would sadly witness another tragic moment in the history of New York City: Hurricane Sandy, which made landfall on the Jersey Shore with hurricane-force winds on October 29, 2012. It caused catastrophic flooding and damage to much of the tri-state area and was the deadliest hurricane to hit the United States since Hurricane Katrina devastated New Orleans and the Gulf Coast in 2005.

Staten Island was hit extremely hard by Hurricane Sandy. "Thousands of houses were damaged, countless cars flipped, people were trapped, and irreplaceable items were lost forever," Jordan Hafizi wrote in the *Staten Island Advance*.

Twenty-four Staten Island residents were killed by the massive storm—"more victims than on any other borough" of New York City, Hafizi reported. Much like 9/11, Hurricane Sandy left behind overwhelming grief that would be permanently ingrained into the minds of every Staten Islander, including Mike.

Mike was relieved that he happened to be on predeployment leave during the storm. He wanted to make sure his parents were safe and be there to help his dad with any possible flooding or damage to the family house. Fortunately, Burbank Avenue didn't sustain damage beyond some flooding.

The morning after the storm hit, Mike got a call from his old friend Jimmy, who was then helping out at the police department. Jimmy told Mike he was going out to one of Staten Island's beaches, which was near the local VFW (Veterans of Foreign Wars) post where Mike's dad had been a member for many years. The plan was to clear debris and search for survivors, and Jimmy was wondering if Mike wanted to help.

"I'll be there," Mike immediately told his fellow former JROTC officer.

The devastation Mike and Jimmy saw at the beach that day was calamitous. Worst of all, the two friends wound up pulling several dead bodies out of the water. Mike never imagined he would experience a tragedy of this magnitude while doing volunteer work between deployments, but, as always, his chief concern was about how the traumatic experience would affect his friend. Jimmy had never seen anything resembling a scene this grim and heartbreaking up close.

Just as Mike had with his father a few weeks earlier, Jimmy broke down in tears as they discussed the harrowing Hurricane Sandy experience later that evening over beers.

"There are certain things you should never have to see and

that you will never forget," Mike told Jimmy. "But when death is staring back at you, there's nothing you can do. You have to find a coping mechanism and move on."

Mike had not only taken his father's advice to heart but was now comforting Jimmy, much like he had Bolivar. Indeed, Jimmy would never forget the horrible aftermath of Hurricane Sandy, but whenever he thought about that day's events, he would hear Mike's comforting voice. That's because his friend wasn't just giving lip service—he truly understood Jimmy's pain and wanted to do whatever he could to help.

Knowing Mike always had their back would help guide Jimmy, Bolivar, and countless others through many moments of darkness in the months and years ahead.

Mike still loved Courtney, but their relationship was on hold as he wrestled with the strains of yet another combat deployment. While they were broken up, he had met a nice young woman named Marissa while visiting his sister Kelly in Maryland. He planned to keep in close touch with both Courtney and Marissa while he was in Afghanistan and sort out what to do next when he got home.

In a sense, Mike felt like his whole life was on hold. While many twenty-three-year-olds were starting to think about getting married, having kids, and saving money for a house, Mike was moving all over the place and essentially living deployment to deployment. He was fully committed to his third combat tour, but a fourth was becoming more and more difficult to imagine.

Despite lingering doubts about his future in the army, Mike accomplished several remarkable feats between Afghanistan deployments. He earned a slot to attend Ranger School and passed all three phases of the grueling sixty-one-day course, which took place at Fort Benning in Columbus, Georgia, and Eglin Air Force Base in Florida.

"I survived the cut, LOL!" Mike posted on his Ranger School

graduation day, July 13, 2012. "Best of luck to Class 07–12. RANGERS LEAD THE WAY!"

Earning the US Army's coveted ranger tab on the heels of two long and difficult deployments might have been Mike's most improbable military achievement. US Army captain Florent Groberg, who earned the Medal of Honor on August 8, 2012, for saving the lives of several fellow soldiers by pushing a suicide bomber away from his patrol, later wrote that surviving Ranger School—not Afghanistan—was the greatest challenge of his life.

"Ranger School challenges everything about a human being," Captain Groberg wrote in his book *8 Seconds of Courage*. "It challenges your mind, your body, your emotions, your leadership, your decision-making, and most importantly, your attitude."

Despite this enormous triumph, Mike wasn't finished. After a celebratory trip about two hours north to Atlanta to go to a baseball game and hit the bars, Mike attended US Army Airborne School, which also took place at Fort Benning.

"Doing the abnormal tomorrow . . . jumping out of a plane while it is still flying!" Mike posted on Facebook on August 5, 2012. "Feet and knees together, LOL."

The three-week Basic Airborne Course, which is referred to as "Jump School" inside the military, culminated with five separate parachute tests.

"One jump down, four to go!" Mike posted on August 6, 2012.

As usual, Mike passed with flying colors and proudly earned his Basic Parachute badge to go along with his new US Army Ranger tab.

"Finally heading back to New York, goodbye Georgia!" Mike posted on August 12, 2012. "Thank you Matney family for all your help."

"Going home tomorrow finally after six months straight of training," Mike would later post as well.

Mike would eventually decide to also pursue induction into the

US Army's prestigious Sergeant Audie Murphy Club, which was reserved for the top 2 percent of enlisted NCOs. It would require a substantial amount of work and studying in addition to his normal duties, but Mike was ready and willing to take on the challenge. "Be all you can be" wasn't just an army recruiting slogan to Mike—it was how he approached his entire military career.

One of Mike's last trips before returning to Fort Drum and then Afghanistan was to Chicago to see his one of his best army buddies, Tino. Mike was thrilled that his friend had mostly healed from the serious injuries he suffered in Afghanistan and was getting ready to start training to become a US Army drill sergeant at Fort Benning, where Mike had gone through boot camp and Ranger School. Tino was equally thrilled about all Mike had accomplished.

"You're in the big leagues now, my friend," Brian said. "But damn it, now I have to go to Ranger School and pass just like you."

Like Jason, Tino was a bit surprised to hear Mike doubting himself despite how well his army career seemed to be going.

"Yeah, okay, I'm a ranger now and everyone thinks I'm this amazing soldier or something," he confided. "But the truth is that I'm not, Tino. I'm just some guy from Staten Island named Mike Ollis.

"I'm not good enough for my guys," he continued while becoming increasingly emotional. "You know better than anyone what Afghanistan is like. These guys need someone better than me."

Stunned and bewildered, Tino tried to both encourage his friend and lighten the mood.

"Are you stupid or something?" he said, quoting *Forrest Gump*. "You've done it all—you're completely prepared. You're going to do just fine as a squad leader.

"Better than fine, actually," Tino continued. "Just remember everything you learned in Iraq, Afghanistan, and Ranger and Airborne Schools. You're going to do great things over there."

Mike appreciated the pep talk even though his doubts remained.

Over and over again while getting ready for his second trip to Afghanistan, the compound attack would enter his mind. While trying not to focus on the sounds of suffocation as his dad had advised, Mike thought about every single detail of the bombing and how to secure an attack site even faster next time.

With so many lives at stake, Mike would never allow himself to be caught off guard during his third combat deployment. Every fiber of his being would be devoted to getting his entire company home safely. Everything else was just background noise.

Mike's final stop before Afghanistan would be Fort Irwin, which has long been the home of the US military's National Training Center. Before heading to Southern California from Fort Drum, Mike went down to Staten Island to say goodbye to his parents, sisters, niece, nephews, family, and friends. He also bid fond farewells to both Courtney and Marissa, while wondering if he would be lucky enough to marry one of them someday after returning from Afghanistan. Either way, Mike intended the end of his third deployment to mark the start of the rest of his life.

As soon as Mike flew out to Southern California before heading back to the country that had haunted his dreams for the past year and a half, almost all those thoughts about his future vanished. For the next eight months, US Army Staff Sergeant Michael Ollis would care only about the welfare and safety of others, not himself.

CHAPTER 10

TRIPLE DEUCE

As had been the case inside his previous units, Mike had quickly endeared himself to the Bushmasters of the US Army Tenth Mountain Division's Second Battalion, Twenty-Second Infantry Regiment. Long before Triple Deuce went to sunny California to complete their predeployment training, the seeds of what would become a tight-knit group of soldiers were planted beneath the frozen fields of Fort Drum in Upstate New York.

Ever since that trip to Pearl Harbor in high school, Mike loved visiting sites of historic military significance. At Fort Drum, he was truly immersed in history while living in an apartment complex on the former grounds of Madison Barracks, which was named after then outgoing president James Madison shortly after the War of 1812. The barracks were built as a direct result of the war, during which Fort Drum served as the army and navy's northern headquarters and prompted the government to realize it needed a permanent troop presence in Sackets Harbor, which overlooks Lake Ontario.

"During its use, Madison Barracks was considered one of the nation's best military posts," according to a history of Madison Barracks posted on the US Army's official website. "A few well-known leaders who spent time at Sackets Harbor were [President and General] Ulysses S. Grant, Gen. Mark Clark, Gen. Jacob Brown, New York City Mayor Fiorello LaGuardia, and President Martin Van Buren." Numerous Medal of Honor recipients once lived at Madison Barracks as well.

Today, Fort Drum houses and trains around eighty thousand active duty and US Army reserve soldiers in a given year. The more than hundred-thousand-acre reservation is one of the army's largest in the lower forty-eight states—and also one of the coldest.

"I finally got my own apartment today! Go me!" Mike posted on Facebook. "I would like to thank my parents for coming up and helping me move in! Love you guys."

Upon his arrival at Fort Drum from his previous 101st Airborne Division assignment in Kentucky, the first thing Mike's newest group of future battle buddies noticed about him was his height. For many members of Triple Deuce, Mike was easily the shortest soldier they had ever served with.

"Oh look, it's Mighty Mouse," a squad leader named Staff Sergeant Brian Schnell said shortly after Mike officially joined his new Tenth Mountain Division unit.

Without hesitation, Mike approached Staff Sergeant Schnell, who not only outranked him at the time but also outweighed him by at least a hundred pounds.

"Oh look, it's the Big Dummy E-6 who's about to get his ass handed to him," Mike said while getting into a wrestling stance. "Are you ready, sir?"

In the middle of their locker room, dozens of Triple Deuce soldiers gathered around to watch what would presumably be one of the quickest wrestling matches they had ever witnessed. At six foot four and about 250 pounds of muscle, Schnell was easily the unit's biggest and most imposing soldier. Compared to Mike, he was André the Giant.

To everyone's amazement, Mike stayed in the fight until it eventually reached a stalemate.

"Have you had enough, Sergeant?" Schnell said as the two soldiers lay on the ground grappling with one another.

"Not a chance, sir," said Mike, despite being caught in a tight headlock. "I'll stay here all day if I have to, sir!"

Exhausted from the unexpectedly stiff challenge, Staff Sergeant Schnell decided to release the headlock and end the impromptu match. Schnell was both surprised and relieved when Mike—whose face was red not from anger but from intense effort—emerged with a smile.

"Good match, sir," he said while patting Schnell on his extremely large shoulders.

"Nice job, Mighty Mou . . ." Schnell responded before catching himself—and his breath. "I mean, Mighty Mike."

"My friends back in Staten Island call me Mikey Muscles," he said with a hearty laugh.

What could have been an ugly fight between Mike and a higher-ranking NCO was instead a bonding experience and just about the best impression Mike could have made on his new platoon. He might have been small, but Mike was also ferocious. Through his postmatch reaction, he had also shown Schnell and the soldiers who were watching that he was a nice guy—unless you made the mistake of mocking his size—who would never shy away from a challenge.

Schnell once again witnessed Mike's tenacity during their first regularly scheduled Thursday ruck march. As Schnell briskly trudged through the snow, he noticed that Mike had started running since he knew it was the only way to keep up with a soldier that was almost a foot taller than him.

"You know you don't have to keep up with me, right Sergeant?" Schnell said. "Feel free to take it easy and fall back."

"Sir, negative, sir!" Mike shouted as his visible breath filled Fort Drum's frigid air.

For six long miles, Mike kept running and finished only a few steps behind Schnell. It was yet another example of how positive and intense of an impression the new 101st Airborne guy was making inside the Tenth Mountain Division unit.

On another ruck march one rainy early spring day, Mike found himself walking through the mud with a younger soldier, Corporal Patrick McTighe. For those six miles, Mike and Patrick carried on a long conversation about their army careers and lives back home. Even though Patrick already knew Mike was a New Yorker due to his thick Staten Island accent, he enjoyed hearing the sergeant's stories about growing up in the city. He was also pleasantly surprised by the NCO's willingness to carry on a friendly conversation with a lower-ranking soldier.

Mike and Patrick also bonded over their family history. When Mike mentioned that his father had fought in Vietnam, Patrick shared that his uncle had done the same. Like Mike, Patrick had been motivated to join the army in large part because of hearing Vietnam stories while growing up. By becoming soldiers, both were living their dreams.

"The one thing I'm not used to is how it always seems to be raining or snowing when we do these marches," Mike lamented to Patrick.

"Well, we have a saying up here at Drum, sir: 'If it's not raining, you're not training,'" Patrick said.

"That's a good one," Mike responded with a big laugh that sounded a little bit like Mickey Mouse. Patrick didn't dare point that out after witnessing Mike's prior showdown with Schnell, though.

After the march, a soldier who had noticed the conversation, Private First Class Eddie Garcia, approached Patrick.

"Yo sir, what's Sergeant Ollis like?" Eddie said.

"He means business," said Patrick. "He's a really nice guy, too."

Another squad leader, Staff Sergeant Doyle Davis, noticed the same attributes in Mike, privately likening him to a fierce chihuahua that would have no problem squaring off with a pit bull. Even before seeing him wrestle Schnell, Doyle could tell Mike was tough and appreciated that he carried himself with professionalism, which he had seen before with former 101st Airborne guys. He also knew that like Schnell and the other three squad leaders, Mike—then an assistant squad leader—had served in Iraq.

Doyle and Mike, however, were the only ones who had served in Afghanistan. Not long after being exposed to Mike's vast combat experience and fierce work ethic, Doyle pushed Mike to pursue a prestigious induction into the Audie Murphy Club. It would require completing a huge seventeen-part nomination packet and then studying for a difficult board exam, but if he himself could tackle the challenge, Doyle thought, Mike definitely could, too.

Doyle also liked how after work, Mike loved to kick back and hang out with everyone, from fellow NCOs to lower- and sometimes even higher-ranking soldiers. After a few drinks one night at Mike's brand-new Madison Barracks apartment, Mike persuaded Doyle, Schnell, and another squad leader to visit the company executive officer (XO), who lived in the same complex. After the beer and liquor they had consumed made it even tougher to navigate through two feet of snow in frigid temperatures, Mike knocked on the XO's door and asked if they could come inside.

As the XO straightened up his place for a minute before letting the freezing and slightly buzzed soldiers in, Mike turned to the three squad leaders.

"Whatever you do, don't say anything about the picture," Mike said while sporting a mischievous grin.

"What picture . . . ?" Doyle started to say before stopping himself as the XO opened the door.

Immediately upon walking inside, Doyle, Schnell, and the other squad leader knew exactly what Mike was talking about. On the wall was a massive painting of a majestic, fully uniformed, classical military figure—with their XO's face painted onto the officer's head.

Doyle started laughing first, followed by Schnell and the other squad leader. Before joining in on the laughter, Mike gently patting his XO on the back and handed him a cold beer he had been carrying in the pocket of his heavy winter coat.

"What are these guys laughing at, Sergeant?" the bewildered captain asked Mike, who responded without fear or hesitation.

"Captain, they are laughing at your fucking painting, sir," he said.

Now, Mike's three fellow soldiers were unable to contain themselves and collapsed to the floor in further and louder howls of laughter. While he was far from amused at first, the XO himself eventually joined in on the fun and wound up having a few drinks and laughs with Mike and his friends.

"You've got pretty big balls for such a little dude, Ollie," Schnell said during the walk back to Mike's apartment.

"Just don't call him Mighty Mouse," Doyle joked before sarcastically thanking Mike for "pissing off" the XO.

By the time Mike left for Ranger and then Jump School, he had developed a strong rapport with the group of squad leaders and most of the forty-two soldiers in his platoon. It was that rapidly developed bond and the respect each of the squad leaders had for Mike that made what could have been a challenging situation while he was away much easier.

As Mike fought through three grueling months of ranger and parachute training at Fort Benning, where he had first earned his place in the US Army ranks six years earlier at boot camp, his platoon learned that one of the squad leaders was being transferred to another unit. It was therefore up to the current squad leaders to recommend a replacement to their superiors.

While meetings between the squad leaders were often lengthy and sometimes heated, that particular discussion might have been one of their shortest. As soon as Mike returned to Fort Drum, he would be given command of his own squad inside Second Platoon, Bravo Company, Second Battalion, Twenty-Second Infantry Regiment of the Tenth Mountain Division. Not long after taking over First Squad, Mike's still-pending promotion to staff sergeant would become official, too.

The other three squad leaders couldn't wait to share the good news with Mike, because they all knew how excited he would be. They were right. Becoming an infantry squad leader had been a goal of Mike's since he was a teenage JROTC cadet. For the twenty-three-year-old sergeant, getting a chance to lead and mentor less experienced soldiers was another dream come true.

Private Eric Patterson was the youngest soldier in the platoon. Like Mike, he joined the army at age seventeen through the army's delayed-entry program with the permission of his parents. He arrived at Fort Drum while Mike was still at Ranger School and had only heard about Sergeant Ollis in passing. While understandably intimidated to be among so many older and more experienced teammates, Eric was excited to meet Mike, especially after finding out that he would become his squad leader upon returning to New York. That was until a few of the soldiers told him a bit more about Mike.

"You know how big Staff Sergeant Schnell is, right?" one of Eric's fellow soldiers said. "Sergeant Ollis is even bigger."

"And he's a lot meaner," another soldier chimed in. "He's six foot seven, about two hundred and seventy-five pounds, and will absolutely smoke you if you so much as stumble during a ruck march or even leave the cap off of your toothpaste."

By the time Mike returned to Fort Drum from Georgia sporting his brand-new US Army Ranger tab, Eric was terrified of his new squad leader. In fact, he was sitting at his locker studying his weapons manual in order to be extraprepared for Mike's arrival when a duffel bag suddenly flew into his space.

"WHERE'S PATTERSON?" someone with a New York accent shouted.

Eric, who stood at attention while simultaneously hoping he wouldn't lose control of his bodily functions, braced for his first encounter with a squad leader who he was told resembled the Incredible Hulk. Suddenly, Mike whipped around the corner and stood directly in front of his face.

"How are you doing today, Private Patterson?" Mike said. "I'm Sergeant Ollis."

There was complete silence as Eric tried to figure out what the hell was going on. The soldier in front of him was five foot nothing and probably wouldn't even crack one hundred and fifty pounds on their locker room scale.

"Respectfully, sir, I don't believe you, sir," Eric stammered.

"ARE YOU QUESTIONING ME, PRIVATE?" Mike shouted. "GET DOWN AND GIVE ME FIFTY PUSH-UPS BEFORE I COURT-MARTIAL YOUR ASS!"

At that moment, everyone in the locker room began to laugh. As it turned out, Mike had heard about the young new soldier during a phone call with his fellow squad leaders while he was still down at Fort Benning. It was then that they decided to play a friendly joke on Eric while letting a few guys in on the joke in order to convince him that Mike was the scariest squad leader in the entire US Army.

Eric breathed a huge sigh of relief as Mike joined in on the laughter and patted him on the back.

"At ease, Private," Mike said. "Just messing around with ya, kid. I know how it feels to be in this spot at your age."

"Sir, thank you, sir," Eric said while wiping sweat off his forehead.

"I'm glad to have you in my squad, Patterson," Mike said before heading over to the squad leaders' office.

After exchanging some high fives, Schnell noticed Mike's brand-new Ranger tab.

"So what should I call you now?" he said. "Tiny Ranger?"

"Oh, you're in for it now, Big Dummy," Mike said, before tackling Schnell for another impromptu wrestling match.

As the soldiers continued their long daily treks through snow and mud in the crisp Upstate New York air, Mike's platoon was quickly developing into one of the finest non–Special Forces fighting units in the US Army. It was becoming such a well-oiled machine that a superior officer bestowed a complimentary nickname on the platoon's four squad leaders: the A-Team.

While grateful for the praise, the four squad leaders naturally had to start arguing about who was which A-Team character. When the dust settled after an animated discussion over beers at one of their favorite watering holes, the 1812 Brewing Company in Sackets Harbor, Doyle was H.M. "Howling Mad" Murdock, Schnell was Bosco Albert "B.A." Baracus, Anthony was John "Hannibal" Smith and Mike was Templeton Arthur "Faceman" Peck. The guys usually referred to him as just Face.

By the time the soldiers of Triple Deuce were given orders to prepare for a combat deployment to eastern Afghanistan's Ghazni Province in January 2013, the squad leaders—and the entire platoon, as a result—were becoming like family. The size of the platoon being reduced from forty-two to thirty-three soldiers in advance of the deployment only added to the already tight-knit atmosphere.

Just as he had been in Staten Island with Jimmy, Rob, Bolivar, Quaseem, Alanna, and Kristen, Mike was the "glue" that held the whole platoon together. If the soldiers in his squad wanted to go out drinking, Mike would often join them and serve as the designated driver. It was a bit unusual for an NCO to go out to the bars with lower-ranking soldiers, but Mike didn't care. The only thing he asked for in return was for one of the soldiers to reciprocate on the few occasions that Mike was in need of a sober driver to get him safely back to base.

When it came to Schnell, Doyle, and Anthony, the Triple Deuce squad leaders were already like four brothers. Not long after returning from Ranger School, Mike went over to Schnell's house to meet his fellow soldier's newborn daughter for the first time. When the door was answered by Brian's wife, Melissa, she began to laugh when she saw Mike standing there with a box of diapers under one arm and a twelve-pack of Bud Light Platinum bottles under the other.

As soon as Mike saw baby Madeline, he dropped everything and asked to hold her.

"Hey there, beautiful!" he said with a huge smile. "You remind me of my little niece Ava."

During another visit to the Schnell house, Mike got his beloved black Ford F-150 truck stuck in the mud. After a few moments of sheer panic, as no earthly possession mattered more to Mike than his truck, he and Schnell managed to push it out. They returned to the house covered in layers of thick mud.

Realizing that his blue jeans were all but ruined, Mike asked Schnell if he could borrow a pair to wear for the rest of the day. While he never had the guts to actually tell Mike, the pair he wound up lending him actually belonged to Melissa. The couple definitely shared a few laughs about it later at their small but strong friend's expense.

Another memorable moment came during a visit to Doyle's house for his daughter's fifth birthday party. Mike had asked Doyle for gift ideas, to which he responded that his little girl loved playing with Barbies. Sure enough, Mike went straight to the local Walmart to buy Barbie and Ken dolls. Mike was so excited to give his friend's daughter the gifts that he showed up to the party nearly an hour and a half early.

With Doyle getting the grill started and his wife busy in the kitchen, Mike asked if their daughter could open her first birth-day present a little early. To Mike and the little girl's delight, the parents granted his request. No one was surprised that she abso-lutely loved her new dolls.

When Doyle came back inside to get something for the grill about twenty minutes later, he and his wife looked at each other and wondered where their daughter and Mike had gone. Sure enough, they were in the other room playing with the new Barbie dolls. Doyle almost fell on the floor laughing at the sight of his tough, unmarried US Army battle buddy sitting on the floor play-ing with dolls in his little girl's Barbie dream house.

"Ollie, you don't have to do this!" Doyle said through laughter. "Come outside and help me with the grill, man."

"It's okay dude, really!" Mike said with a smile. "I have a niece and grew up with two sisters—do you know how many of these dolls I've been forced to play with over the years?"

A split second later, the doorbell rang. Sure enough, Schnell was standing outside. Even though he had a newborn daughter of his own, Mike knew that he would never live it down if Schnell caught him playing with Barbies.

"Shit, it's Schnell!" Mike said while instantly dropping the doll and running toward the kitchen. "Quick, someone get me a beer!"

Triple Deuce's last large-scale training exercise before deploy-ing to Afghanistan was at the US military's National Training Center in San Bernadino County, California. The differences be-tween Fort Irwin's Mojave Desert terrain and the frigid moun-tains of Fort Drum were obvious, but as Mike explained to the younger soldiers in his squad, they would experience similarly stark changes in Afghanistan once winter gave way to the Taliban's notorious spring and summer fighting seasons.

Even though he didn't talk about his first deployment to Af-ghanistan that often, it comforted the younger soldiers in his squad—especially now eighteen-year-old Eric—to know that their squad leader had already been there. The fact that he didn't go into every detail about what happened during his deployment actually increased the respect many inside the platoon felt for Mike. After all, the soldier who told the fewest war stories was often the one who had seen the most action.

The men of Triple Deuce participated in many simulated skirmishes and large-scale battles during their time in southern California. As Mike's squad patrolled up a hill during one scorching summer day in the Mojave Desert, the soldiers walked straight into a machine gunner's nest that was being manned by a rival army unit. The ambush shocked Private First Class Eddie Garcia, who fell backward when the "enemy" soldiers began firing hundreds of blanks.

Before Eddie could blink, Mike had already yelled "CONTACT!" and started directing him and the rest of the squad into their respective fighting positions. After they held their own and instructors declared an end to the battle, Eddie told the squad's youngest soldier, Eric, that he had never seen anyone react faster during a firefight than Staff Sergeant Ollis. To both young soldiers, it was insane how quickly Mike could flip a switch upon realizing his men were in grave danger.

The scariest situation Mike experienced at Fort Irwin involved his close friend Doyle. During a training mission, Doyle accidentally rolled his Humvee down the side of a mountain, prompting an immediate reaction from Mike, who grabbed Schnell and headed outside to jump into the first military vehicle he could find to go help his friend.

"That's a negative, Staff Sergeant," Mike's commanding officer said. "You and Staff Sergeant Schnell need to stay here."

Mike instantly recalled the helpless feeling of being confined to a guard tower in Afghanistan while his close friend Tino's MRAP was engulfed in fire and smoke after striking an IED. There was no way he was going to let something happen to Doyle, especially with him and Schnell perfectly capable of embarking on a rescue mission. In that moment, Mike didn't care about anything other than helping Doyle, least of all the rank of the US Army officer standing in his way.

"With all due respect, fuck you, sir," Mike said as almost everyone around him gasped. "That's my friend and I'm going out there to help him!"

Despite potentially disastrous consequences for his career, Mike followed through and wound up receiving no punishment other than a tongue-lashing when he got back. Even if he had been brought up on charges, everyone acquainted with Mike knew that he would have barely batted an eye. After all, he was just fulfilling perhaps the most important seven words in the US Army Ranger creed, which he had spent many hours memorizing at Fort Benning: "I will never leave a fallen comrade." All that mattered to Mike was Doyle being okay, which he was.

When the soldiers of Triple Deuce returned from California to Fort Drum, they had a few weeks to say their goodbyes and get their affairs in order before trading the mountains of Upstate New York for the cliffs of eastern Afghanistan. While Mike knew that the cardinal rule of any combat deployment was to expect the unexpected, he constantly reassured his squad that their many months of training had prepared them for this moment. As long as everyone did their jobs and trusted one another, everyone would make it home to their families in one piece.

Before the soldiers left for what was supposed to be eight months of battling al Qaeda and the Taliban in Ghazni Province, they received an early January 2013 visit from a decorated US Army veteran who had fought and bled for his country during wartime: Bob Ollis. He had traveled up to Fort Drum to drive Mike's truck back to Staten Island and—most importantly—say goodbye to his son.

Upon meeting Bob, the other squad leaders and soldiers instantly knew where Mike's friendliness and fierce dedication to the army had come from. When a few of the guys asked Bob about his heroics in Vietnam, he told them he was just doing his job and only wished that everyone else made it home safely.

"Keep your heads up over there, believe in each other, and I'll see all of you later this year," Bob told the soldiers of Triple Deuce. "Michael's mom and I couldn't be prouder of each and every one of you."

Before Bob headed back to Staten Island, Mike gave his father a huge hug and jokingly threatened him with a punch in the nose if anything happened to his truck while he was overseas. Then he told his father that he loved him.

"I love you too, Michael," Bob said while admiring his son's new Ranger tab, which he knew took a massive amount of courage and fortitude for his son to earn. "You're a good boy and a great American soldier."

During the drive from Sackets Harbor back to Staten Island, Bob suddenly began to cry. He had watched his only son leave for war in the past, but for some unexplainable reason, this time felt different.

"Please don't hurt him, Lord," Bob said while driving his son's truck down a snowy Interstate 81. "Hurt me."

CHAPTER 11

STAY READY

W ell, time for round three!" Mike posted on Facebook as his unit departed Fort Drum on January 19, 2013. Five days later, he posted about his platoon's long journey overseas.

"Had the best flight of my life to Afghanistan flying in a C-17 in the cockpit flying over the mountains," he wrote before changing his profile to a picture of a 2012 visit to the Vietnam Veterans Memorial in Washington with his dad.

As soon as the massive C-17 aircraft touched down at the largest American base in Afghanistan—Bagram Airfield—US Army Staff Sergeant Michael Ollis was all business.

"Okay, we're here," Mike said to the soldiers in his squad upon arriving in eastern Afghanistan, where they would join the war effort as part of Regional Command East, which was commanded by Mike's former 101st Airborne Division under the umbrella of NATO's International Security Assistance Force (ISAF). "Let's go—it's time to do our jobs."

As the calendar turned to 2013 in Afghanistan—the twelfth year of the US-led war against al Qaeda and the Taliban—the painstaking progress Mike and thousands of fellow American troops and veterans had helped bring about was now squarely in the spotlight. Despite widespread skepticism that crossed party lines, the White House and NATO allies were still clinging to President Obama's pledge to withdraw all combat troops from Afghanistan by 2014.

In a special report for *USA Today* on February 2, 2013—about two weeks after the soldiers of Triple Deuce arrived in Ghazni Province to start their deployment, Carmen Gentile wrote about conditions on the ground in Ghazni's Muqur district and eastern Afghanistan as a whole. As had been the case while serving in Kandahar in 2010 and 2011, Mike served on the central front of what had already become America's longest war:

> Eastern Afghanistan will be the greatest test of that transition. US Marines and Army soldiers succeeded in vanquishing Taliban fighters from the strongholds in the south in campaigns lasting years in Helmand and Kandahar Provinces. Rather than reinforce the south, the Taliban attacked to the east, where fighters from militant-infested northwest Pakistan bolstered their forces.
>
> US forces responded last year by shifting troops to the east, intensifying efforts in Ghazni to combat a persistent enemy as a deadline issued by President Obama closes in for US troops to withdraw.
>
> Ghazni is an important thoroughfare for the Taliban and other militant groups in eastern Afghanistan. The country's main route, Highway 1, runs through this market halfway between the country's two largest cities, Kabul and Kandahar. Just off the highway are vast stretches of barren crop fields covered in winter frost and surrounded by snow-topped mountains.
>
> Winter is typically when many Taliban fighters return to Pakistan to rest and re-arm for the spring. But this winter the Taliban remained active, perhaps to test the strength

of the Afghan forces that have taken up positions turned over by the US military.

Polish forces were leading the NATO effort in the province. The arrival of US troops and Afghan soldiers kept the Taliban out of the bigger population centers. But some locals say the Taliban is still firmly in control of most districts and just waiting for US forces to leave so they can take on the Afghan forces left behind.

"They didn't bring the security, the weather did," says Abdul Kaim, waving a bony finger at the American forces in the market as he explained the recent snowfall is what stopped the fighting by making it too hard for either side to travel.

Lieutenant Colonel Jeremy Schroeder disagreed and said the region was secured well before winter's arrival.

"I guess that's a good problem," says Schroeder, interpreting the Taliban's willingness to brave the cold months in Afghanistan as a sign the militants are concerned about losing too much ground to NATO and Afghan forces come spring. "It means you are having success."

As they settled in right next to the crucial Highway 1 at Combat Outpost Muqur, some soldiers inside Triple Deuce had a less rosy and far more blunt assessment of the conditions in Ghazni Province. Not only was their base in a potentially dangerous position, but everything from the housing to the guard towers seemed to be poorly constructed.

"You know what the best part about living in a tent in Afghanistan is?" Mike posted on Facebook on February 3, 2013. "When it snows, your tent collapses on you, LOL."

"I thought I told you to ask for an upgrade in your accommodations," Linda jokingly wrote in a response that Mike subsequently liked. "You never listen to your mom."

Eventually, the frequent jokes about the awful living conditions turned to frustration for many of the soldiers of Triple Deuce.

"This is a clusterfuck," Doyle told Mike early in the mission. "I don't know what the hell we're even doing on this shithole FOB except to help out the ANA [Afghan National Army]."

Knowing that Doyle was the only squad leader other than him to complete a previous deployment to Afghanistan, Mike could speak candidly to his fellow squad leader about what might transpire during the difficult days ahead:

"You know better than anyone how it works over here, Mad Dog," Mike said, using Doyle's A-Team nickname. "Nothing will happen for a few months and then all of a sudden the enemy will hit us with everything they've got."

Doyle nodded his head in complete agreement. As all four squad leaders would convey to their men throughout the ensuing months, staying vigilant would be the key to the entire deployment. As Doyle and Mike knew from their previous stints in Afghanistan and reading intelligence reports, letting your guard down—even for a few moments—was precisely how an entire squad could get wiped out in a sneak attack by an enemy notorious for hiding in the shadows.

Despite the larger-than-usual Taliban presence, Ghazni Province was nevertheless ice cold—literally and figuratively. While the mountain warriors of Triple Deuce were accustomed to frigid temperatures at Fort Drum, the wind whipping off the desolate snowcaps of eastern Afghanistan somehow felt even more vicious. The bleak conditions combined with the fact that fighting had ground to an almost complete halt made many of the soldiers—especially the younger guys—feel isolated, depressed, or sometimes just flat-out bored.

That's why Mike and the other squad leaders were almost constantly running mass-casualty drills or more mundane tasks like having the soldiers clean their weapons.

"It might not always seem like it when things get slow, but make no mistake: we are at war over here," Mike told his squad. "Remember your training and trust each other. Most importantly: Stay focused and *always* stay ready."

"Yes, sir!" the soldiers in Mike's First Squad responded in unison.

To Mike, staying ready also meant always trying to become a better soldier. When he had some downtime, Mike would work on his Audie Murphy Club application and study for upcoming exams. He would encourage the soldiers under his command to do the same, including Eddie, who he had been promoted and elevated to assistant squad leader in the months leading up to the deployment.

"Yo, Garcia, didn't you say you want to be a sergeant someday?" Mike said.

"Yes, sir," Eddie said while putting down a magazine and taking off his headphones.

"Well then, why aren't you studying?" said Mike. "The army doesn't just hand a sergeant's rank out to random soldiers. You have to earn it."

"I know, sir," Eddie said with a soft but audible sigh. "To be honest, I just don't feel like it right now."

Before he could finish his sentence, Eddie saw the disappointment on Mike's face and immediately began feeling guilty about his laziness. Almost every time he walked past his squad leader's bunk, he had seen Mike studying hard for the Audie Murphy Club evaluations. Eddie then quietly braced himself for the pushback that he knew was coming from his squad leader.

"Little Migo, you are going to get your ass out of bed and become a sergeant in the United States Army," Mike said. "You will study hard and do well on the sergeant's test. That's an order. Do you understand me, Corporal?"

"Yes, sir," Eddie said before cracking the books. While he

would have preferred to keep listening to music and reading his magazine, Eddie later realized that his squad leader—who had affectionately bestowed the Little Migo nickname on him while they were training together back at Fort Drum—genuinely wanted him to succeed.

As for Mike's studies, he wasn't just working on his Audie Murphy Club packet. He had also started taking online courses at Ashford University, which is now known as the University of Arizona Global Campus. He aced his first class, Personal Dimensions of Education, and carried a 4.0 grade point average throughout his deployment. Even in the cold, rugged mountains of eastern Afghanistan, Mike was always trying to better himself.

While Mike's fellow soldiers did the best they could to fill the time, the fact that Triple Deuce was initially stationed on such a remote combat outpost that held little strategic value (in the opinion of at least one squad leader) only added to the strange, uneasy feeling that was slowly spreading through the platoon. They had all just spent more than a year in chilly Upstate New York training to fight terrorists and help the Afghan people. It was therefore natural for each soldier to wonder about the platoon's mission and when it would finally get into full swing.

"Deployment is quiet," Mike wrote to his friend Brian Constantino, who was starting his new job as a drill sergeant at Fort Benning. "We're really just packing shit up and closing bases."

"Any new ladies you're talking to?" Tino wrote to Mike in a subsequent Facebook message.

"Nah, I've been too busy with this [Audie Murphy Club] board and dealing with equipment turn in," Mike replied. "I'm closing this FOB down, leading my squad and getting my team leader and medic ready for the [promotion] boards."

When he wasn't studying or helping others do the same, Mike often passed the time by—naturally—wrestling with the much bigger squad leader, Staff Sergeant Schnell. On one particularly dreary day, the soldiers decided to put on riot gear that was in storage in case the FOB was attacked by Taliban fighters or by a mob of angry Afghans. Not since the most recent *WrestleMania* had a crowd of young men been so entertained by two guys beating the living hell out of each other. Mike and Schnell both had a blast listening to cheers as they rolled around in the dirt calling each other Tiny Ranger and Big Dummy.

As winter slowly began turning to early spring, conditions on COP Muqur somehow got worse. Every single time it rained, the base would flood and essentially become a mud pit. Running drills and exercising were more difficult in the mud, which added to the sense of boredom and isolation. Dozens of soldiers had to share a scant few computers and phones (assuming that they were even working correctly on a given day), which made communicating with their loved ones back home extremely difficult during those early months in eastern Afghanistan.

When the official order eventually came to fully tear down and evacuate COP Muqur, Mike and his fellow soldiers were more than happy to oblige. The men of Triple Deuce couldn't wait to reach their next destination, FOB Warrior, which was only about twelve miles to the west of their current position along Highway 1. Once they tore down and handed over the remnants of COP Muqur to the Afghans, they could start doing more of what they had trained to do in Afghanistan: going outside the wire on patrol and fighting the bad guys.

With the teardown of COP Muqur came another milestone moment in Mike's military career. Despite some uncertainty leading up to his third combat deployment, particularly as he considered his potential future with Courtney, Marissa, or whomever he wound up settling down with when he got home, Mike had made a landmark decision while deployed to a war zone for the second time in three-plus years and the third since 2008.

In those seemingly hopeless hills of eastern Afghanistan, Staff

Sergeant Michael Harold Ollis managed to inspire the soldiers in his squad and just about the entire platoon by raising his right hand and swearing to defend his country for another six years. Until at least February 2019, Mike would still be doing his dream job of being a soldier in the United States Army.

"Well, I signed up for six more years!" Mike posted with a smiley face on Facebook on February 16, 2013. "Starting today!"

Following the promotion ceremony, Mike turned around and saluted the large American flag that his fellow soldiers were holding.

While it's hard to know his exact reasoning, whatever doubts had crept into his mind before the deployment had been erased by returning to Afghanistan, commanding a squad during wartime, and pursuing induction into the prestigious Sergeant Audie Murphy Club.

Mike was missing his family and friends more than usual on this deployment, though. Whether because of the desolate conditions or the natural effect of a third combat tour in five-plus years, he couldn't wait to complete his mission and go home.

"After this deployment, I'm actually going on a vacation!" he posted on Facebook on February 19, 2013.

"Let us know when you're in New York," Maureen Ollis replied. "We'll come to see you. Stay safe, we'll see you then!"

"Hey Aunt Maureen, I will," Mike responded. "Tell Uncle Tommy I said hello."

Around this time, Mike also placed a phone call to his father. After first making sure that his son was safe, Bob asked Mike about his decision to reenlist and how he was feeling about his future.

"I feel good about it, Dad," he said. "I'll feel even better when this deployment is over and I'm hanging out on the back porch with all of you."

After ripping down COP Muqur and heading west, Mike settled into what was supposed to be his job throughout this particular deployment: leading soldiers onto the battlefield. He also enjoyed having more amenities at FOB Warrior than he had at the miserable COP Muqur.

"Shower after two weeks and Snapple in a can," Mike posted on Facebook shortly after his platoon arrived at FOB Warrior. "I'm really happy right now, LOL!!!"

When Mike's squad left the comforts of their new FOB to go outside the wire on foot, Mike insisted on positioning himself at the very front of the formation. When they went on patrol inside armored personnel carriers, Mike was always inside the lead truck, which was equipped with the army's latest mine-roller technology mounted on the front. He had spent countless hours training himself and others to operate the massive complex vehicle and was grateful to be using his skills to help protect his fellow soldiers from enemy land mines and IEDs.

"These are designed to blow up," Albert Bacon, a civilian contractor, explained about the updated mine-roller technology in a December 12, 2011, article published by the US Army.

"It's a good piece of equipment," added Specialist John Rollins of the army's 548th Transportation Company. "It does its job."

"That job is detonating improvised explosive devices, or IEDs, before soldiers drive over them," the article continued. "The rollers are one element in the deadly serious effort to defeat IEDs."

"I feel safer and I know everyone behind me is safer," said Private First Class Juan Callepiedrahita.

About a year and a half after that article was published, the soldiers of Triple Deuce undoubtedly shared similar feelings while patrolling the same perilous terrain. It wasn't just because they had a mine roller, though. It was because of the soldier who was always in command of the enormous vehicle: Staff Sergeant Michael Ollis.

"I lead the way on every patrol, LOL," Mike wrote to his buddy Tino in a June 2013 Facebook message. "I love it."

"Hell yes!" Tino replied.

"I'm always lead truck," Mike added.

"I loved being 1st squad leader," Tino wrote back. "Same reason."

"Yeah, it's fun," Mike responded. "Team leader and squad leader are the best jobs I've had so far."

The fact that Mike enjoyed his job didn't mean it was any less dangerous—even while completing routine tasks.

"Why is it that every deployment I bang my head and get a new scar?" Mike joked in a March 5, 2013, Facebook post before explaining that he was struck by a pole while putting up a tent. "It's not like I was doing anything cool."

It wasn't just his willingness and eagerness to lead patrols that gave the Triple Deuce soldiers so much collective confidence in Mike. It was his unparalleled ability and willingness to facilitate repairs on machinery and equipment that made him the platoon's go-to guy whenever something needed a quick fix. Mike, who had first started out helping his dad repair newspaper trucks as a young kid in New York, was now servicing multifaceted military vehicles in the middle of a war zone. It made him proud.

Mike was also the lead operator for Second Platoon on the CROWS (Common Remotely Operated Weapon Station) missile system. From his position inside a heavily armored vehicle, Mike could acquire and fire at targets at rapid speed and devastating precision. Since he was certified on the CROWS system, Mike utilized downtime at COP Muqur and then FOB Warrior to train soldiers both inside and outside his squad on how to use the complicated remote battle station.

"I know what you're thinking: it's like playing a video game," Mike would tell the younger guys during CROWS classes he organized for soldiers on both bases. "But always remember that this is real life. If you're sitting here screwing around or don't follow the training I'm about to give you, a lot of innocent people could get injured or killed."

Eventually, Mike's prowess on the CROWS and mine-roller

technology became so well-known that soldiers from other companies would come to FOB Warrior to take one of Mike's classes. It didn't take long for him to gain a reputation as the best mine-roller and CROWS operator in the Tenth Mountain Division's entire Second Battalion. Considering that as many as a thousand soldiers made up an average army battalion, Mike had earned extremely high praise.

Whenever Mike went outside the wire, he led from the front and always tried to keep his soldiers focused and calm. Sometimes that even included his fellow squad leaders, as on one day when Mike and Schnell began taking enemy fire while moving around equipment and directing traffic.

"Contact!" Schnell yelled over his radio before telling Mike he was moving his squad to a position closer to the gunfire.

Before his friend and fellow squad leader moved his men, however, Mike delivered a blunt message, albeit slightly tongue-in-cheek.

"Don't you go and get yourself killed now, BA," said Mike, using Schnell's A-Team nickname. "Melissa's gonna be pissed at you if you die, and I'll kick your ass even worse than I did while wearing that riot suit."

"You're right about Melissa," Schnell said with a smirk. "Not so sure about the second part though, Face."

During another patrol with Schnell, Mike accidentally got the mine roller stuck in a huge pit of mud. It instantly reminded both soldiers of the time Mike's truck got stuck back at home. Since it was the one and only mistake Mike ever made with a mine roller in Afghanistan, Mike knew he would never hear the end of it. He was right.

"That thing is a lot bigger than your Ford F-150, Ollie!" Schnell joked.

"Shut the fuck up and help me, man!" Mike replied with a laugh.

Throughout his time in the army, Mike had a unique way of delivering (and receiving) serious messages with just enough humor to make it impossible for someone to stay mad at him. Even when he got into impassioned arguments with his fellow squad leaders, which happened often because all four of them cared deeply about taking care of the soldiers under their command, everyone always seemed to know that Mike's intensity came from a noble place. When things got testy, Mike would be among the first to extend his hand and make peace.

Nobody saw Mike's ferocious dedication from a closer vantage point than Schnell and Doyle, who was mentoring Mike during his studies for the Audie Murphy board exams. Almost every night after completing their guard shifts, Mike and Doyle would reconvene inside one of FOB Warrior's Vietnam War–style B huts—short for "barracks huts," which was essentially cheap, temporary base housing. For the next two and a half to three hours, Doyle would quiz Mike on the intricacies of being an elite US Army NCO and give him tips on what the board might ask during his upcoming round-robin question-and-answer session, which would be conducted via satellite phone since Mike was deployed to Afghanistan.

While helping him study, Doyle saw not only a supremely qualified NCO but also a soldier who was pouring his heart and soul into every aspect of the Sergeant Audie Murphy Club nomination and examination process. When the big day arrived in April 2013, Mike was ready to face the board and answer their many complicated and wide-ranging questions.

"Yo, Ollie!" Doyle said after Mike emerged from FOB Warrior's mobile welfare and recreation tent, where there were phones and computers available for use. "How did it go?"

"We'll see," Mike said with a shrug. "Either way, thanks for all your help, Murdock."

"Anytime, Face," Doyle said.

Doyle would soon leave FOB Warrior to help start a new platoon. At first, Mike's heart sank as he recalled Tino's reassignment to a different company on the 2010–11 deployment to Kandahar. This time around in Afghanistan, however, Mike continued to see and work with Doyle on a regular basis, for which both NCOs were grateful.

By the middle of 2013, it was clear that the war in Afghanistan would not be as deadly for American troops as it was during the three preceding years, during which a combined 1,223 US service members had made the ultimate sacrifice, according to icasualties .org. While the 2013 American death toll would wind up being less than half that of 2012, Mike had spent more than enough time in Afghanistan to know that statistics meant next to nothing. At every waking moment, he had to be ready to lead his troops, whether it was during a small skirmish or a large-scale battle.

"If someone is a threat, we *will* defend ourselves," Mike would frequently tell soldiers in his squad.

A photo of General George S. Patton that Mike posted from Afghanistan on May 6, 2013, expressed the same sentiment.

"May God have mercy on my enemies, because I won't," the caption said.

Mike's readiness was on full display during one seemingly routine patrol to set up a target for a Special Forces unit that needed to conduct artillery tests. For a lot of soldiers, it was boring busy-work, especially since they weren't even the soldiers who would get to "zero" (set the sights) of their powerful weapons and blow things up.

"Seriously, this is what we're doing?" Eddie said under his breath. "Come on."

"You want to be a sergeant someday, right?" Mike said. "Well, this is the job, Corporal. And make sure to study when we get back to the FOB or I'll have no choice but kick your ass, Little Migo."

Even though Eddie had technically just been reprimanded by a superior, Eddie once again felt reassured that his squad leader knew what the hell he was doing out on the battlefield. Mike's nudging pushed him to look for the best in every situation and become a better soldier.

As the sun set behind the mountains of eastern Afghanistan one evening, Mike's and Schnell's squads were coming back from a route-clearance mission when they noticed a suspicious man in the valley. He was moving slowly and awkwardly and seemed to be looking down at an object on the ground, which immediately raised all kinds of red flags related to a possible IED. He ran away as soon as he spotted American soldiers moving toward him.

Eventually, the presence of an IED was confirmed, prompting Schnell to call an explosive-ordnance-disposal (EOD) team to safely dispose of the roadside bomb. After Schnell's and Mike's squads returned to FOB Warrior, however, a soldier manning the guard tower reported that a similar-looking man was moving back toward the valley. When Schnell and Mike took respective looks using their binoculars, it was clear not only that the suspicious individual was a "spotter" but also that he was actively trying to detonate the IED using some sort of remote device.

Knowing that the EOD team was on the way and that the roadside bomb could potentially explode right as they arrived on site, Mike quickly assembled a small squad that jumped in an armored vehicle and raced out toward the spotter. Knowing that an IED was buried close by and could easily go off in the next few minutes didn't faze Mike at all. Heading toward the danger and putting himself in harm's way to shield others was his job. There was no way he was going to let some EOD guy get killed instead of him.

As it turned out, the spotter once again ran away as Mike's truck raced toward him and, for whatever reason, the IED never blew up. It was then safely disabled by the EOD team before anyone was hurt. Were it not for Mike's bravery and quick thinking, the outcome could have been different—and tragic.

During another mission to set up a target, Mike's Triple Deuce squad encountered a man who appeared to be a goatherd. While Eric, Eddie, another soldier and their interpreter didn't give more than a passing thought to the seemingly harmless local Afghan or his goats, Mike's previous deployments had taught him to never assume anything while outside the wire.

"Hey, man, my men and I are working here, so I'll need you to move your goats," Mike said through the interpreter. The man offered no response.

After a few moments of awkward silence, Mike had the interpreter ask him again.

"I'm not moving," the interpreter translated, prompting Mike to slowly put his finger on the trigger of his rifle.

Following some more strange silence, the goatherd looked at Mike, who was beginning to suspect that he could be a terrorist in disguise.

"Hey, let me have that pen sticking out of your pocket," the man suddenly said through the interpreter.

Mike obliged before speaking back up about thirty seconds later.

"So, are you moving?" he said.

"No," the goatherd said.

"Well, then, can I have my pen back?" Mike replied as his soldiers quietly chuckled.

"No," the goatherd repeated. "Give me your watch and then maybe I'll move."

As Mike moved the interpreter backward in case the man had a bomb or hidden weapon, he decided to turn up the figurative temperature. The literal one was already much hotter than when his squad arrived in Afghanistan, and Mike was tired of seeing his soldiers sweating in a random field while having their mission slowed down by a purported goatherd who apparently had a death wish.

"Okay, tell him this," Mike said to the interpreter. "Not only am I not gonna give him my fucking watch, but if he doesn't get his ass moving, he and his goats are gonna die. It's as simple as that."

The man and his goats did finally start moving, but very slowly and not enough to give Mike's squad ample room to start setting up their targets. When the nearby Special Forces unit subsequently radioed to ask what was holding things up, Mike started to get pissed off.

"A goatherd?" the SF soldier replied on the radio. "Well, someone tell him to move!"

Mike was not normally aggressive with Afghan or Iraqi civilians. He sympathized with the fact that they were caught in the middle of a long war after many years of mistreatment, intimidation, and outright brutality by the Taliban and al Qaeda. He was known for being friendly and funny while visiting children in local bazaars and medical clinics. He also always took extra time to listen to the concerns and complaints of local tribal elders. Most of all, Mike loved the food the villagers would sometimes cook for his squad, which included the best lamb kabobs any of the soldiers had ever tasted.

"Okay, everyone, back to the FOB," Mike shouted after his initial efforts to move the goatherd had failed. "Time to cook some goat kabobs!"

As soon as they returned to FOB Warrior, Mike decided to fire a rocket in the direction of the goatherd, who had gone from a passerby to a possible threat. Mike had no intention of hurting him, however, having aimed the rocket at a target that was nowhere near far enough to hit him or his goats. Sure enough, the ensuing explosion put some pep in the goatherd's step.

"You can keep the pen!" Mike yelled as the uncooperative

Afghan and his now-frightened goats hightailed it away from the US Army squad's area of operations.

In addition to admiring his quick-witted sense of humor and the extreme sense of confidence he instilled while leading patrols, whether inside trucks or out on foot, Mike's soldiers loved the care packages that would arrive from his friends around the country, his parents in Staten Island, or the elementary school classes Kim taught in New Jersey. Mike's B hut always seemed to have the best stuff, whether it was candy, magazines, or even toothpaste.

"I want to give you a compliment, Face," Schnell said. "In one of the poorest, most primitive countries in the world, you might have the whitest set of teeth."

"Thanks, BA," Mike said while continuing to brush. "You know I've got to keep this smile bright and ready for the ladies when we get home!"

Mike always made sure to thank whoever mailed him the latest care package that he and his squad were enjoying.

"Hello Amy, thank you for mailing a package to me. I'm very excited!" Mike wrote on May 9, 2013, to the wife of his close army friend. "Tell Jason I said thank you as well, but if the package sucks I'm going to throw it in the burn pit, LMAO! Just kidding, I'm going to like it."

Even though he felt the love from back home, Mike couldn't help but miss the little things about being in New York, even if just being able to crack open a beer and watch a ballgame.

"Really wish I could watch a Mets game," he posted on May 10, 2013.

A few weeks later on Memorial Day 2013, Mike commented on a photo posted by a friend, Ann Gregory, that showed his niece and nephews participating in the annual Staten Island Memorial Day parade.

"I miss the family," he posted on May 27, 2013. "Thanks for the pic."

A few weeks later, Mike's parents, sisters and their families were on a family vacation to Rehoboth Beach, Delaware, when the deployed soldier called them from Afghanistan via FaceTime. While Mike was initially frustrated that a poor internet connection prevented him from seeing Bob, Linda, Kim, Bill, Kelly, Dave, and the kids, he was relieved that he could at least hear them. On the flip side, Mike's family was thrilled that for whatever reason, they could see and hear Mike perfectly.

During the call, Mike told his family that if his Audie Murphy Club application was approved, he could potentially come home early. As Mike was well aware, however, plans frequently change while deployed to a war zone.

"Don't bother planning a homecoming party this time," he said.

After hearing how everyone's summer was going and expressing particular interest in his nephew William's summer travel soccer season, it was seemingly a good time for Mike to say goodbye and carry on with his duties. Perhaps because he was growing increasingly homesick, Mike didn't want to hang up.

"Just keep talking," he told his family. "I miss you guys so much."

By late June, being stuck in Afghanistan was starting to wear even further on Mike and his fellow soldiers.

"I'm doing alright, but this place sucks, LOL," he wrote to Amy on June 27, 2013. "I'm hoping we can all hang out when I'm on leave after this deployment. I'll let you know when I get leave."

As the calendar flipped to July, when temperatures in Ghazni Province typically averaged about eighty degrees, it was time for yet another pivotal moment in Mike's military career. On Independence Day 2013, a letter signed by a US Army command sergeant major (CSM) was mailed from FOB Warrior. The letter's subject was "Memorandum SAMC [Sergeant Audie Murphy Club] Selection Board, Letter of Recommendation, SSG Ollis, Michael":

I strongly recommend SSG Ollis for Sergeant Audie Murphy Club induction. I have been his CSM for nine months and can personally attest to his discipline, intelligence, fortitude and professionalism. I have observed SSG Ollis over the past five months while at FOB Warrior and COP Muqur. During that time, he has consistently impressed me with his tactical and technical knowledge along with his leadership skills. His soldiers, as well as his peers, confirm his exceptional qualities as a leader, trainer and motivator.

SSG Ollis lives the values of what this prestigious club represents daily. As squad leader, he has distinguished himself by putting the needs of everyone above his own, never faltering when others needed his help or advice. SSG Ollis is the embodiment of professionalism and leads by example.

SSG Ollis would be a phenomenal choice for this honor and I recommend him wholeheartedly and without reservation.

> *James L. Manning Jr.*
> *CSM, USA [US Army]*

A little over a month later, a Sergeant Audie Murphy Club acceptance letter arrived at FOB Warrior addressed to Staff Sergeant Michael Ollis, who was due to celebrate his twenty-fifth birthday in just two months. Indeed, the hard work Mike had been putting in since starting JROTC nearly a decade earlier had culminated with his being recognized as one of the very best noncommissioned officers in the United States Army.

"I guess we've got to start calling you Ollie Murphy now," Schnell said to Mike with a smile before picking him up in a bear hug. "Congratulations, brother."

There were a lot more people Mike couldn't wait to tell, but two stood out. One was Doyle, a fellow Audie Murphy Club member who had pushed him to apply for the award while they were training together at Fort Drum and helped him study, even in the sometimes miserable conditions of eastern Afghanistan.

"Welcome to the club, brother!" Doyle posted on Mike's Facebook timeline on August 10, 2013, after talking on the phone with Mike.

"Thanks bro," Mike wrote in what was his last Facebook post or comment of the deployment.

The other person Mike couldn't wait to share the good news with was his father, who he knew would be proud of his son for working his absolute hardest to reach even greater heights.

When he returned to Fort Drum from Afghanistan, Mike would receive a bronze medallion and a powder-blue ribbon, which symbolizes the official color of the infantry. He would then be able to wear the medallion at military balls and other functions requiring a dress uniform. A bronze carving of the legendary Audie Murphy—a Medal of Honor recipient and the most decorated US Army soldier of World War II, who also received awards from France and Belgium—appeared on the front of the medallion. OUTSTANDING NONCOMMISSIONED OFFICERS was carved on the back, along with the US Army staff sergeant insignia.

The Sergeant Audie Murphy Club's motto was simple, yet it was perfect for Mike: "You lead from the front." It was a quote from Audie Murphy himself that Mike had been living out while constantly training and deploying to war zones since becoming a soldier almost seven years earlier.

"You did it, Michael," Bob told his son over the phone. "Your mother and I couldn't be any prouder of you. Make sure to be careful over there, son."

"I will, Pop," Mike said.

Mike also did his best to keep in touch with his sisters in conversations that were usually over Facebook Messenger.

"Hey, how's Jersey?" Mike wrote to Kim from FOB Warrior on August 3, 2013.

"Good! Crowded, but fun!" Kim responded. "How are you? When are you coming home?"

"I'm good," Mike replied. "I'll be home around September. Send my best to Bill and the boys. The kids are getting big."

"Will do!" Kim wrote back. "Miss you!"

A few weeks later, Mike asked Kim for her new address in New Jersey, which she promptly provided.

"Thanks," Mike wrote on August 9, 2013. "I might mail stuff of mine to you because mom and dad won't be home when it gets to the States."

Mike was referring to a trip to Europe their parents were planning with friends. He knew they would be away and didn't want boxes of his personal items to be sitting on their front porch for the several weeks it would take Mike to get a ride down to Staten Island from Fort Drum, where Triple Deuce would be returning that September.

Not so fast. Just as the squad leaders received orders to fully tear down and evacuate FOB Warrior, much like they had done at COP Muqur, they got some disheartening news. At the height of Afghanistan's 2013 summer fighting season, the soldiers of Triple Deuce learned that their Second Platoon was the only one operating in all of Ghazni Province to be selected by the army for a deployment extension.

Instead of heading back to Fort Drum in early September, Mike and his fellow soldiers wouldn't be going home until late October. The platoon was collectively devastated. Mike was particularly annoyed since he and a few friends had been planning celebratory homecoming trips to Las Vegas and possibly even Mexico.

"This fucking sucks," Mike vented to Jimmy, one of his oldest friends from back home, upon getting the bad news. "I couldn't wait to celebrate my birthday with all of you guys."

"It's okay, buddy," Jimmy said. "It just means we'll have to celebrate twice as hard when you get back. In the meantime, I'll send you another care package.

"Stay safe over there, man," Jimmy added. "The Bud Lights will be on ice when you get home!"

As he prepared to spend his twenty-fifth birthday in Afghanistan instead of drinking, barbecuing, and sitting in the hot tub in his parents' backyard in New Dorp, Mike tried not to let the disappointment he was feeling rub off on his squad. His soldiers had never experienced a full deployment, let alone an extension, which meant they were taking the news even harder than he was. After taking some time to himself, Mike gathered the squad for a pep talk.

"I know you're all disappointed and pissed off," Mike said to his soldiers. "It's a fucking bummer—there's no way around that. But here's the good news: once we finish tearing down this FOB, we get to stop at FOB Ghazni for a few days on our way to FOB Shank, which is over in Logar Province. FOB Ghazni is run by the Polish army and has a nice gym, big chow hall, and huge MWR center full of phones and computers for you to call, message, and Skype with your parents, buddies, and girlfriends."

Mike noticed that Eddie, Patterson, and other soldiers in his squad were starting to nod their heads. While it would indeed suck to spend their deployment's additional month at FOB Shank— one of the most frequently rocketed American bases in all of Afghanistan—at least they would get to stop at FOB Ghazni and relax for a few days first.

Life on FOB Warrior had been mostly quiet for the past few months other than some indirect rocket fire. Mike had made sure to keep his soldiers ready by running those mass-casualty-attack drills, but as his squad helped a skeleton crew of American soldiers tear down the decent-sized FOB, secure its equipment, and hand what was left of the base over to the Afghans, it was hard not to let complacency creep in. Mike occasionally found his thoughts drifting to enjoying the relative luxuries of FOB Ghazni, where he planned to hit the gym hard before rewarding himself with big and delicious meals in the chow hall.

Those plans changed when Mike injured his leg while repairing the mine roller on his platoon's lead truck in preparation for the armored convoy to FOB Ghazni. The injury wasn't that serious, but it was nevertheless extremely frustrating to Mike since it meant he wouldn't be able to fully enjoy having a nice gym to work out in. It was another huge bummer in what seemed like a developing pattern of bad news.

The night before Triple Deuce was scheduled to leave FOB Warrior, Mike's squad was responsible for guarding the base's gates and manning its guard tower. The skeleton US Army crew left on the almost fully torn down FOB hoped for a quiet evening of alternating naps and watch shifts before formally handing Warrior over to the Afghans the next morning.

All of a sudden, the Triple Deuce soldiers were jolted by the sounds of rocket-propelled grenades and small-arms fire landing inside their base. Seemingly out of nowhere, FOB Warrior was under attack by approximately twenty-five to thirty Taliban fighters.

"My squad will take QRF [quick-reaction force]," Doyle said over the radio to Mike before leading his soldiers to the other side of the base.

"Roger that," Mike said. "Schnell and my squads will hold our ground here."

Mike, Schnell, and several of their soldiers were up in the guard tower when they suddenly started coughing. A few terrifying seconds later, they could barely breathe. Unbeknownst to either squad leader at the time, a few Special Forces soldiers in charge of defending the base during a large-scale attack had launched several smoke grenades filled with CS gas toward the insurgent fighters. What the SF soldiers didn't fully take into account, however, was that heavy winds would blow the tear gas right back toward their base. Mike and Schnell's guard tower was the first spot inside the FOB to suffer the consequences.

Once their coughing and breathing problems subsided, Mike, Schnell, Doyle, their soldiers, and their SF counterparts were able to successfully repel the attack without any American casualties being suffered. Still, the incident was concerning to Mike and his fellow squad leaders. After several months of relative calm, the Taliban seemed emboldened and ready to confront the Americans head-on throughout the summer fighting season's conclusion.

What Mike had initially hoped would be a relatively relaxing few days at FOB Ghazni did not turn out that way once they left FOB Warrior on the heels of the previous night's attack. Upon arriving at their temporary base, which—as Mike had told his men—was under the command of the Polish armed forces, Triple Deuce's squad leaders felt uneasy. Not only was FOB Ghazni operated by a foreign army, but things seemed just a bit too calm and routine to the four battle-hardened squad leaders, each of whom was serving their third respective combat deployment.

"I don't like this, BA," Mike said while shaking his injured leg to keep it loose.

"Me neither, Face," Schnell said. "This is not good."

The squad leaders had valid reasons to be concerned. While FOB Ghazni was certainly well guarded, the surrounding area had become increasingly volatile, as military analyst Bill Roggio explained in the Foundation for Defense of Democracies' *The Long War Journal* as August 2013 drew to a close:

> With the transfer of control from the coalition to Afghan
> security forces and the drawdown of coalition personnel,

violence in Ghazni Province has spiked. So far in August, the Taliban have kidnapped a female member of parliament and two other civilians in the province, and then later offered to exchange the captives for eight Taliban fighters currently in prison. The Taliban have also kidnapped and then executed eight other civilians in Ghazni. Additionally, a Polish soldier was recently killed in a Taliban attack.

The Afghan military and police claim to have killed 36 Taliban fighters in Ghazni since August 18. But in one of the reports, which said that security forces killed 20 Taliban fighters, the police admitted that four police personnel had been killed and policemen had abandoned several outposts during a Taliban assault.

Ghazni is a known Taliban and al Qaeda hub in the southeast. Senior Taliban, al Qaeda, Lashkar-e-Taiba, and Islamic Movement of Uzbekistan commanders are known to operate in the province.

As Mike and the Triple Deuce soldiers tried to settle in despite the danger, Schnell would soon be flying to Afghanistan's largest American base—Bagram Airfield—to pick up equipment and transport it over to their next landing spot, FOB Shank. The other three squads, including Mike's, would therefore spend the next few days on FOB Ghazni with minimal ammunition.

Almost immediately upon arriving at the bulky FOB, where they found out they would likely be staying for just three days, all of Second Platoon's soldiers received a safety briefing from one of the Polish soldiers who spoke English. He was flanked by a US Army Green Beret officer who explained that there was a heavier-than-usual Special Forces presence at FOB Ghazni due to a change of command that just happened to be taking place over those few days. Having twice as many Green Berets at the FOB immediately made almost everyone breathe a bit easier.

The biggest takeaway from the safety briefing, however, was what to do if an attack took place.

"Squad leaders: you have one responsibility," the Green Beret said. "Get your men to your assigned bunker and stay in place until our QRF teams clear the FOB. Don't go out there and try to be heroes—let us SF guys do our jobs."

"This is an international base," the Polish officer chimed in. "That means there are a lot of foreign soldiers here, including from the Afghan National Army. If there's an attack, we don't want the wrong people getting killed."

Despite some initial trepidation by the squad leaders, the Polish army seemed competent in its leadership and management of the base. About a year and a half before Mike and his fellow soldiers arrived, then deputy defense secretary Ash Carter, later appointed secretary of defense by President Obama, had personally visited FOB Ghazni and—according to a 2012 story by Sergeant First Class Tyrone C. Marshall Jr.—praised Polish military forces after finishing his inspection of the base:

> "Thank you very much . . . to the Polish contingent here," Carter said. "You've been great partners right from the very beginning, and we are admiring of your professionalism and dedication."
>
> Polish military leaders told the secretary they are working very closely with coalition troops from other nations, and there is a "very good partnership with US forces in the area."
>
> The group talked about logistics, building capacity in the area, construction and other operational issues. Following their discussions, Carter re-emphasized that the union between U.S. forces and Polish troops serves as "a great, great partnership."

Leading up to Triple Deuce's August 26, 2013, arrival at FOB Ghazni, there had been some intelligence chatter about a possible suicide vehicle–borne improvised explosive device (SVBIED) attack being planned on convoys outside the base. Since there were no plans for any outside-the-wire missions involving Mike or his fellow Tenth Mountain Division soldiers, however, the warnings didn't seem to have much relevance.

In fact, Mike and his squad would—for the most part—have nothing to do for the next three days. Their only responsibilities were to rest and eat well. If they chose, they were all free to work out at the gym or call their loved ones back home from the MWR center as long as they had advance approval from their superiors.

Ghazni was bigger than the relatively large FOB they had just come from—Warrior—and full of the amenities that Mike had talked up to his squad. The tents were bigger, the food tasted better, and the internet connection was faster. There was also a shopping bazaar that certainly wouldn't have been found on FOBs like Warrior or Muqur. For Mike and the other Second Platoon soldiers, it was refreshing to simply walk around, browse the shops, and hang out. For at least three days, life was supposed to be good for the soldiers of Triple Deuce.

As for the military infrastructure, there was no fixed-wing aircraft strip, but the base was full of numerous helicopter landing pads. The walls and guard towers surrounding the FOB were massive—so tall that the soldiers almost felt as if they were underground while walking through the base's sandy, fortified interior, which was filled with Hesco defensive barriers. In case of a mass-casualty terrorist attack, there were not only the series of bunkers that Mike and the other squad leaders were informed about during the briefing but also two top-of-the-line medical facilities managed by the Polish army and the US Air Force, as a 2013 article by Staff Sergeant Stephanie Wade explained:

All over Afghanistan, service members are deployed to forward operating bases as they continue their mission to train and assist Afghan forces. Currently, a team of 24 airmen with a range of medical specialties are deployed to FOB Ghazni as the only Air Force Forward Surgical Team in Afghanistan.

On FOB Ghazni, there are two medical facilities to treat trauma patients, the Polish field hospital and an Air Force FST. Both hospitals provide care 24/7 to US service members and coalition forces. The Polish hospital is a fully-equipped hospital and can keep patients overnight if need be, while the FST is a role two facility that specializes in stabilizing patients in order to facilitate their travel to a higher level of care.

Even though Mike was keenly aware that no forward operating base in Afghanistan or Iraq was ever fully secure, American, Polish, and Afghan soldiers on FOB Ghazni seemed to have every reason to feel relatively safe. Mike and the other squad leaders continued to warn against complacency, however, while telling soldiers under their command to check in every hour on the hour and always move around in teams of at least two men. Should anything go wrong on the FOB while Triple Deuce was there, the soldiers' orders were crystal clear: get to the nearest bunker.

At the MWR during his first day on FOB Ghazni, Mike messaged on Facebook with his close friend from back home, Kristen, as well as Marissa and Courtney.

"I'm in Hilton Head this week with Alanna, Jimmy, Rob and Quaseem," Kristen wrote.

"Oh man, I'm so jealous," Mike replied. "Tell everyone I say hey.

"When you get back to Staten Island, can you mail me some

White Castle burgers?" Mike continued before telling Kristen he had to let another soldier use the computer.

"I don't think those would taste good, but I promise we'll all hit up the White Castle when you get back!" Kristen replied.

"I'm gonna hold you to that," Mike wrote. "Okay, I gotta go. Be careful."

"YOU be careful!" Kristen responded. "Bye Mike, we all miss you!"

Later in the day on August 26, 2013, Mike messaged with Marissa.

"What's up?" he wrote to Marissa.

"Laying at the beach, how about you?" she replied.

"Nice, just checking email," he responded.

"Don't you come home soon?" Marissa inquired.

"October," Mike wrote. "I'll have two weeks off in November and then a month off in December."

"I feel like you've been there forever," Marissa responded.

After chitchatting back and forth, Marissa asked Mike about his postdeployment plans.

"Aren't you moving to Florida?" she said.

"Maybe," he replied. "I'll find out in December."

Before leaving FOB Warrior, Mike had applied for a job at Eglin Air Force Base on the Florida panhandle, where he would train recruits during the sixteen-day third phase of US Army Ranger School, which he had completed about a year and a half earlier. In addition to the prospective job, Mike apparently had another good reason for wanting to settle down in the Sunshine State.

"I want to retire at 37," wrote Mike, who was less than three weeks from turning twenty-five.

"Definitely dreaming big," said Marissa, with whom Mike would also wind up having a Skype call the next day from the MWR center.

"I can do it, though," Mike responded. "When I'm 37, I'll have 20 years in the Army!"

The following day, Mike had a conversation with Courtney that was also focused on the future. After hearing him lament his leg injury and cursing his deployment extension, Courtney—whom Mike still deeply cared about—asked him to give some serious thought to the next chapter of their relationship. Courtney was starting her medical residency and wondered if Mike would be ready to make a longer-term commitment once he returned from Afghanistan.

"I need to know what your plan is," Courtney said.

"So do I," Mike said. "Believe me, I can't wait to get home and start the rest of my life."

As Staff Sergeant Michael Ollis went to sleep inside a tent on FOB Ghazni in eastern Afghanistan on the night of August 27, 2013, during his third combat deployment in seven years, the music shuffle on his black iPhone landed on one of his favorite songs by one of his home state's favorite sons, Billy Joel. The song was "Goodnight Saigon"—which instantly reminded him of his dad and the Father's Day tribute he had painstakingly put together throughout Mr. Kielty's seventh grade history class:

> We promised our mothers we'd write.
> And we would all go down together.

Would the next day on FOB Ghazni be boring and uneventful or the defining moment of Mike's life and career as a US Army soldier? Only God knew the answer to that question. All Mike could do was stay ready and mentally prepare himself—and the soldiers under his care—for the unknown.

No matter what wound up happening on August 28, 2013, Mike had spent the entire deployment determined that the soldiers of Triple Deuce would *not* "all go down together." If a situation arose that required someone to put himself in harm's way to ensure everyone else's safety, Mike would be the first to volunteer and—as Sergeant Audie Murphy once said—lead from the front.

CHAPTER 12

BĘDĘ PILNOWAŁ TWOICH PLECÓW

August 28, 2013, was the final day that Staff Sergeant Michael Ollis would spend on FOB Ghazni in the rugged mountains of eastern Afghanistan. That night, Mike, his squad, and their fellow Second Platoon soldiers were set to fly to Bagram Airfield and link up with Schnell, who was on the huge American installation to deal with supply issues. Once the equipment problems were sorted out, Triple Deuce would head to Logar Province to finish up their ten-month deployment at FOB Shank.

Despite still being annoyed by being the only platoon to have its deployment extended, Mike and the members of his squad were in a relatively decent mood that day. The skies were clear, it wasn't too hot, and—best of all—they had virtually nothing to do. Their only assigned responsibility was to be ready for their midnight flight to Bagram, which meant they could sit around all day playing video games, watching movies, listening to music, and even taking naps if they felt like it. Mike had different ideas, at least for the soldiers in his squad.

Before heading to FOB Shank, where the internet and telephone connections might not be as stable, Mike thought it was important for him and his men to Skype, message, or call their loved ones that day. After eating breakfast and doing a lighter-than-usual morning workout due to the minor leg injury that was still slowing him down, Mike went to see his platoon's first sergeant to request some extra time at the MWR center for the soldiers in his squad. After asking why and being satisfied with Mike's explanation, the first sergeant granted the request.

"Yo Patterson, come with us to the MWR," Mike said to Eric outside his tent.

"No thank you, sir," Eric said. "I just talked to my family last night, so I'm good."

"Roger that," Mike said. "Make sure you get some rest—we've got a late flight tonight."

"Yes, sir," Eric said.

About an hour later, a soldier from Schnell's squad, Shane Leo, approached Eric's tent. With his squad leader away at Bagram, Shane was bored and wanted to go to the MWR to message with some friends and family back in Michigan. After initially telling Shane that he had already turned down his own squad leader's invitation, Eric changed his mind and decided to walk over to the MWR with his fellow soldier. While he didn't plan to make any calls, Eric figured that hanging out with his army buddies would be more entertaining than sitting alone in a dusty tent.

When they arrived at the MWR center—a wooden structure that resembled a small one-story house—Eric noticed that Staff Sergeant Ollis was talking on the phone. Indeed, Mike had placed a call to his dad's cell phone, knowing that he would be with his mom as they vacationed with friends in London.

To the frustration of both Bob and Linda, there was a lot more static than normal during this particular phone call. The background noise was so loud that it made it almost impossible to make out exactly what their only son was saying—except at the very end of the call.

"I love you, Mom," said Mike, who was nearly shouting inside the MWR. "I love you, Dad!"

"We love you too, Michael," Bob and Linda shouted back in unison just as the choppy call cut out. "Stay safe!"

It was about 1545 (3:45 p.m. Afghanistan time) when Mike finished making his phone calls—just over eight hours before his platoon's scheduled flight to link up with Schnell at Bagram. For the next few minutes, Mike decided to relax on a dusty wooden bench inside the MWR center and have a conversation with Eric, who had already told him earlier that he didn't have any calls to make that day.

After some chitchat about what was going on in their respective hometowns in New York and Texas, Mike and Eric began talking about heading back to their tents and trying to take naps before their late-night flight to Bagram.

BOOM.

All at once, the MWR center began to shake amid some of the loudest sounds a human being's ears could possibly withstand. The front doors of the MWR flew open, suddenly filling the entire building with thick smoke and sand. The lights immediately cut off, and every computer screen went black. Mike and Eric were simultaneously blown off the wooden bench they were sitting on and violently thrown backward.

After a few terrifying moments that resembled a scene from the World War II movie *Saving Private Ryan*—where every external event seemed to be taking place in slow motion—Mike rose up from the rocks and debris he suddenly found himself covered in and gave the loudest command he had shouted since the deadly compound attack in Sangsar, Afghanistan, just under three years earlier.

"GET TO THE BUNKER!" Mike ordered everyone inside the suddenly dark MWR center, which was shaking so hard it felt like it was on the verge of crumbling.

While he wasn't sure if an enemy rocket, mortar, or perhaps even an SVBIED had caused the earth-shattering explosion, the gunfire Mike soon heard coming from outside only meant one thing: FOB Ghazni was under attack.

"FOLLOW ME!" Mike yelled while leading his men out of the building and toward the bunker, which was a few yards from the MWR center.

What no one could have known for certain was that at 1554 local time on August 28, 2013, a truck carrying more than three thousand pounds of explosives had slammed squarely into FOB Ghazni's eastern perimeter wall, which was only about one hundred and fifty yards from the MWR where Mike, his soldiers, and some civilian contractors were sitting. Seconds later, Taliban fighters positioned outside to the east, west, and north began bombarding the base with mortars, hand grenades, RPGs, and machine-gun fire. Some insurgents were shooting down from mountains and a nearby hotel, while others were firing from right outside the gates.

To the south, another powerful explosion had just gone off about five hundred feet from FOB Ghazni's perimeter wall. While not much made sense in those first few moments, it was now abundantly clear that this was an all-out enemy assault that would consume hundreds of American, Polish, and Afghan soldiers on the large base—as well as the civilian contractors—for the next several hours.

Nobody who was on FOB Ghazni that day would ever forget what Mike, Eric, and the other soldiers saw next. As soon as they escaped the smoke- and dust-filled MWR center, they were looking up at the largest mushroom cloud any of them had ever seen. The fiery, rapidly darkening formation was ominous, surreal, and terrifying. In a few seconds, a beautiful, relatively quiet late-summer day had become fully consumed by pandemonium and horror.

Mike knew there was no time for his soldiers to stand there

gazing at the mushroom cloud that suddenly towered above them. From the moment the explosion first knocked him over, it was as if a switch Mike didn't know was inside of him suddenly flipped to the on position. Perhaps it was because he had already experienced an attack that began with a startling explosion. Either way, Mike knew exactly what to do this time around.

Once the soldiers and a group of five contractors who had been inside the MWR safely reached the nearby bunker, Mike took count of the soldiers and asked the civilian workers if everyone in their group was accounted for. Even though he was pretty sure nobody was left behind in the MWR, Mike knew that in a life-or-death situation, assumptions weren't good enough. In Mike's mind, the safety of every soul inside that bunker and MWR center was now his responsibility.

"Patterson and Leo, I need you to follow me," he ordered the soldiers. "Let's clear the MWR front to back and make sure that nobody's left in there."

About three minutes later, Mike, Eric, and Shane safely made their way back over to the MWR despite multiple fires burning, debris blowing everywhere, and fierce gunfights beginning to erupt near the blast site. In the early stages of what would become an enormous battle, the base's perimeter walls were being defended primarily by Polish soldiers, many of whom were standing on makeshift platforms with their rifles poking through barbed wire. In those frantic first few moments, the overriding mission was to prevent any terrorists from breaching the base through a suddenly gaping hole in the perimeter wall.

Even as Mike, Eric, and Shane became surrounded by many more secondary explosions, thick black smoke, and unrelenting gunfire, it was a relief—and somewhat of a miracle—that nobody inside FOB Ghazni's MWR center had been seriously injured or killed by a three-thousand-pound bomb that had detonated a mere one hundred and fifty yards away. Due in large part to the

Polish soldiers defending the perimeter, the three American soldiers also didn't encounter any enemy fighters while checking the now-collapsed and dust-filled MWR for survivors.

Once he and his men safely returned to the bunker, Mike then began coordinating the security plan with Eric, Shane, and another squad leader who was inside the bunker, Anthony. They did so over the screams of several civilian contractors, who were understandably frightened by the fierce battle that had erupted so quickly and unexpectedly all over FOB Ghazni. After trying to calm down the workers and giving a new set of orders, Mike abruptly said something to Eric that took him by complete surprise.

"I'm going over to the platoon sergeant's tent to give him an up," Mike said. An "up" was confirmation that everyone in Mike's group was safe and accounted for.

The first thing Eric did was tilt his head downward to see what Mike was wearing. He had no helmet or body armor on and was wearing only his standard US Army digital camouflage fatigue jacket and pants. He was also without a radio. Mike was carrying his M4 carbine assault rifle, at least.

At the same time, Eric was well aware that since the platoon had been dealing with supply issues that Schnell was at Bagram to help solve, Mike was only carrying one magazine. If Mike left the bunker, he would do so with no protective gear, no communication devices, and just thirty bullets to defend himself.

"No, sir," Eric said. "I either go out there with you or you're staying here."

"What was that, Patterson?" Mike said with surprise.

"I said no, sir," said Eric, who was becoming visibly upset. "You always told me that we move in battle teams! Nobody goes out alone."

"This is my call, Private," Mike said. "I'm your squad leader and it's my job to give the orders right now."

"Fuck that, Ollie!" Eric shouted while temporarily dropping "sir" from his vocabulary.

"If you go out there, you're going to die."

Even as the gunfire outside the bunker grew louder and louder, Mike managed to take a deep breath and put his arm around the panicked eighteen-year-old soldier, who had never experienced a battle anywhere near this scale in his still very young army career. Despite his initial abrasion at being given orders by a private, Mike realized that Eric was genuinely concerned about the safety of his squad leader.

"I'm not going to die," Mike spoke as softly as possible given the tremendous amount of noise outside. "I'm just going to give our platoon sergeant an up.

"I need you to stay here and take charge—I taught you everything you need to know to get the job done," Mike said.

After witnessing the end of Mike and Eric's argument turned reconciliation, Shane—whose squad leader, Schnell, had landed at Bagram Airfield just six hours before the attack—decided to chime in.

"Shouldn't we come with you, Sergeant Ollie?" Shane said.

"That's a negative, Corporal," Mike said. "You stay here with Patterson and help keep the others calm. I'll be back."

After nodding at Shane and giving Eric a quick hug, Mike ran outside and straight toward the nearest sounds of gunfire. A few soldiers inside the bunker who didn't see or hear his exchanges with Eric or Shane amid the bedlam didn't even realize Mike had left the bunker until a few minutes later.

Mike knew that Eric was correct in saying that they were supposed to move in battle teams, but having been through the Sangsar attack, he also knew this situation was different. If a young soldier like Eric went outside the bunker with no body armor and only thirty rounds, it would mean almost certain death. While there had been a few skirmishes and indirect fire incidents with the enemy during the previous seven-plus months, the vast majority of Second Platoon was experiencing their first large-scale firefight.

The fact that Mike was a battle-hardened, ranger-qualified soldier with nearly three full combat deployments under his belt meant he should at least have a fighting chance. If anyone in that bunker was going to get hurt or die that day, Mike wanted it to be him. The stench of gunpowder, burning materials, and thick smoke only deepened Mike's resolve not to let this day end with him pulling more dead or gasping soldiers from the unforgiving wreckage of war.

On August 28, 2013, on a secure base turned chaotic battlefield in eastern Afghanistan, the moment Staff Sergeant Michael Ollis had spent most of his childhood and his entire adult life preparing for had arrived. Completely ignoring the leg pain that had hampered his ability to run for the better part of a week, Mike began what would wind up being an all-out sprint through an international military base that had become a full-scale combat zone.

While deciding where to run first, Mike ultimately chose the most dangerous spot on the entire base: the still-billowing mushroom cloud. FOB Ghazni's eastern perimeter gate was about a football field and a half away from the bunker where his fellow soldiers were now relatively safe and shielded from the unrelenting violence he was now witnessing. As the thick black smoke billowed, Mike initially flinched when what looked like small orange pockets of fire began exploding within the cloud. He had never seen anything like it.

As his eyes moved downward, Mike saw those Polish soldiers firing down from a guard tower and the top of the wall toward what he soon realized was the gaping hole in the once heavily fortified, barbed wired eastern perimeter. The crater was huge—approximately forty-two yards wide. As he took cover and crouched into a firing position, Mike then saw a small group of

US Army Green Berets shooting at what initially looked like an Afghan National Army soldier.

By August 2013, Mike had spent about twenty total months in Afghanistan and fifteen in Iraq. He didn't need an expert to tell him what was going on: terrorists disguised in ANA uniforms were now pouring into FOB Ghazni to conduct further attacks on American, Polish, and Afghan soldiers and civilian workers. As Mike's Casio Digital G-Shock wristwatch read 1600 (4:00 p.m. local time), an already terrible situation was rapidly descending into disaster.

To protect his soldiers and everyone on the FOB, Mike resolved to do whatever he could to prevent the fake ANA soldiers from penetrating the base. Without blinking, Mike raised his M4 carbine rifle and began firing.

Staff Sergeant Doyle Davis had quickly gotten his squad to the nearest bunker after the first explosion had shattered the relative peace inside their tent. While the first few moments were confusing, it didn't take Doyle long to realize—like Mike, who had been much closer to the explosion—that FOB Ghazni was under attack.

A sobering, scary message that was initially delivered in Polish over the FOB's emergency-alert loudspeaker system confirmed Doyle's worst fears.

"Enemy combatants have breached the wire," the now English-speaking voice said in a thick Polish accent. "We have enemy insurgents with suicide vests and AK-47s."

A critical part of the message was then translated in multiple Afghan dialects.

"If you are an Afghan National Army soldier, lay down on the ground NOW with your hands on your head," the voice said.

Doyle now knew what Mike had witnessed at the explosion site: Taliban or al Qaeda fighters wearing ANA uniforms were inside the base.

What Doyle and Mike didn't know was that not only were the insurgents wearing suicide vests under those ANA uniforms, but because of numerous traitors that the Taliban had planted on the base to spy on coalition troops, the terrorists were carrying detailed maps of FOB Ghazni that included locations of every single bunker in addition to the MWR, gym, chow hall, and other populated base facilities. The situation was grave, and the terrorists had to be stopped at all costs.

While Doyle was focused primarily on keeping his young soldiers calm and keeping the bunker safe, his mind briefly wandered to his close friend Mike, who he knew was inside the MWR when the explosion occurred. As he heard gunfire popping in the distance, there was no doubt in Doyle's mind that Mike was exactly where he always wanted to be: squarely in the middle of the fight.

Eddie, who was Mike's assistant squad leader but had stayed in his tent to study instead of going to the MWR, was in a different bunker with a fellow corporal, Patrick McTighe. They had also heard the announcement—an "alamo call," as they later called it—about enemy fighters breaching the base. Just as they had been trained at Fort Drum and throughout the mass-casualty drills the squad leaders had been running throughout their Afghanistan deployment, they had quickly put on their body armor, grabbed their weapons, and gotten into defensive positions.

The first few minutes were pure anarchy, with near-constant gunfire and explosions all around them. It got even scarier when a wide-eyed American soldier ran into the bunker, identified himself, and then told them that terrorists disguised as Afghans were running all over the FOB and starting to blow themselves up.

"Don't trust anybody wearing an ANA uniform!" one of the soldiers said while trying to catch his breath.

As enemy RPGs began to land closer and closer to their bunker, Eddie thought not only about his own safety but also about the well-being of his squad leader. Patrick was also thinking about Mike, but even more so about Eric, who was his best friend in the army. While they had no idea if anyone had been killed in the initial explosion or ensuing firefights, the only thing they knew for sure was that if Staff Sergeant Ollis was anywhere near the action, their brothers-in-arms should have a good chance of surviving the enemy assault.

Then US Army Staff Sergeant Earl Plumlee was on the opposite side of FOB Ghazni when the first two explosions rocked the base. After initially running to the south side, Earl realized that the perimeter had *not* been breached by the second powerful bomb, which he later learned detonated early because of the valiant actions of a group of alert (and real) ANA soldiers before the SVBIED could reach the wall.

Satisfied with the ability of the Polish army's ability to man guard towers and even tanks to defend the south side of the base, Earl and a small group of fellow SF soldiers jumped in a Toyota pickup truck and drove toward the mushroom cloud on the east side. What happened over the next hour would forever change the lives of Earl and everyone who fought beside him.

Second lieutenant Karol Cierpica, a junior officer in NATO's International Provincial Reconstruction Team, had just finished a workout and walked back to his Polish army living quarters when he heard the first explosion. After initially believing it was a rocket attack outside his barracks, Karol knew the situation was even more serious after seeing the burning black mushroom cloud climb into the once bright afternoon sky. Once he saw his fellow Polish soldiers and civilian contractors rushing into a bomb shelter, Karol knew what he had to do next to keep them safe: run toward the giant cloud of dust in the sky.

Karol, who was wearing only shorts and a T-shirt, soon realized that the eastern wall had been breached and that total mayhem had ensued as he heard a deafening series of blasts caused by RPGs, hand grenades, mortars, and exploding suicide vests. Considering that there was constant gunfire with shouting mixed in, it was by far the most chaotic scene that Karol—who was in the middle of his third Afghanistan deployment—had witnessed. Karol knew he needed not only to get more equipment but also to tell the others what was going on.

After warning his fellow troops and grabbing a helmet, pistol, and bulletproof vest, Karol linked up with five other Polish soldiers and began firing at insurgents trying to enter the base through the smoldering blast site. After shooting at several suspected terrorists, Karol separated from the group to gain a better vantage point and then was hit by shrapnel from a nearby explosion.

Since he was wearing shorts, Karol could clearly see that the leg wound wasn't serious. Without hesitation, the Polish soldier bravely returned to his feet and rejoined the fight.

Karol ran around for approximately two minutes before ending up near a fence. There, he encountered a young-looking US Army soldier who was trying to push forward and get himself into a better position to help defend the base. While seeing an American counterpart didn't surprise Karol, his appearance most certainly did. He was carrying an M4 rifle, but nothing else—no grenades or additional ammunition. Even more astonishing was that the soldier, whose face was covered with dirt and black smoke residue, wasn't wearing any body armor. He didn't even have a helmet to protect his head.

A few seconds later, Karol was face-to-face with the US Army soldier as they moved into position about fifty yards away from a series of Connex shipping containers. They were trying to reach an area that appeared to be a much better vantage point to defend the base than their current location, which was inside a narrow lane near a bullet-riddled all-terrain vehicle and the Toyota pickup. At the time, neither of them knew the pickup had been previously occupied by US Army Special Forces soldiers.

The narrow lane directly faced the breach in the wall, which was about one hundred yards away but was being blanketed by enemy machine-gun fire as insurgents fired into the base. To reach the shipping containers, Karol and the American soldier would first have to run as fast as they could through the increasingly rapid machine-gun fire.

While briefly turning around looking into the American man's blue eyes, Karol felt a strange but significant sense of camaraderie and confidence. The soldier's facial expression was serious, but also as friendly as someone could be under such extreme circumstances. Even while surrounded by a whirlwind of gunfire, explosions, and yelling, Karol felt like he knew exactly what the American—whom he didn't recall ever meeting on the FOB—was trying to communicate when he suddenly raised both hands and started pointing in the Polish soldier's direction.

Będę pilnował twoich pleców, Karol believed the American was trying to tell him. *I will watch your back.*

Just before encountering Karol, Mike had been sprinting through the hellish battlefield despite his nagging leg injury. During those few agonizing minutes, Mike saw things no human being should ever see. What he experienced during the Sangsar attack and Hurricane Sandy were horrific, but August 28, 2013, on FOB Ghazni was probably even worse.

Much of the dusty, smoke-filled landscape was now littered with body parts: arms, legs, and even torsos. The pieces were so badly charred that it was almost impossible to identify who had been killed or—in some cases—if the remains were even human. Several soldiers who saw the same harrowing images as Mike would later be treated for post-traumatic stress (PTS).

Did the body parts belong to enemy fighters, coalition soldiers, or perhaps some of Mike's American friends? Undeterred by the unknown, Mike ran toward the sounds of danger at a speed similar to his high school JROTC running drills on the Petrides School's track. That's when he first encountered second lieutenant Karol Cierpica and gave him the look and hand signal that the Polish soldier would never forget.

Mike crouched down and provided cover fire for Karol as the Polish soldier successfully navigated the narrow lane facing the breach in the perimeter wall. Braving machine-gun fire, Mike then made it through as well.

When Mike rounded the corner, the walled-in American unmanned vehicle service center, which was called the Copperhead UAV Compound, was to his immediate right. He then passed a parked Gator ATV vehicle and a Hesco barrier before darting between the Toyota pickup on his left and an empty water tank on his right.

That's when Mike and Karol suddenly saw a group of four American special operators, including US Army Green Beret Staff Sergeant Earl Plumlee.

Earl had already seen several fellow American soldiers wounded and expended nearly all of his ammunition in the ten terrifying minutes since the first explosion. He had already killed several suicide bombers before seeing their vests either immediately blow up or start burning like blowtorches as they lay dead in the dust. One had been shot right outside a bunker near the breach and another only a few yards from there.

Body parts of five dead terrorists were strewn all around the area where Mike, Karol, Earl, and three other service members were now positioned, which made fighting even more difficult since they had to worry about suicide vests possibly exploding all around them. If they wanted to survive, it was crucial to stay as far away as they could from the dead bodies.

Except for two bullets, Earl had just run out of ammunition and asked a chief warrant officer to replace him at the front of their patrol when he heard a voice.

"Hey," Mike yelled to Earl. "Can we come with you?"

"10–4," Earl shouted. "Got any ammo?"

"Not much, but that's affirmative!" Mike shouted with a grin.

Earl, who was making sure to keep a close eye on where he was walking in addition to looking for more bad guys, managed to take a quick glance back at Mike. He was probably about twenty-five or thirty yards behind the Green Beret and also walking behind Karol, whom Earl hadn't noticed at first.

After also realizing that Mike wasn't wearing any protective gear, Earl gave him a quick nod. Having just almost completely run out of ammunition, it felt good knowing that someone had his back.

The chief warrant officer, a Navy SEAL, Earl, and his fellow Green Berets were moving south across a concrete taxiway that was near two more Connex shipping containers and a box of equipment. Karol was behind them and had just taken his first few steps onto the taxiway. Mike was in the rear, having just walked past the empty water tank, an electrical junction box beside the Copperhead UAV compound, and then a pallet box. He had not yet reached the taxiway, as Mike was scanning for threats while—just as he had promised—carefully watching the backs of his Polish counterpart and the Americans in front of him.

The time was 1601 when someone suddenly yelled "GRENADE!"

A terrorist wearing an ANA uniform who had been lying on the ground after being shot suddenly sat up and—as if he was playing basketball—bounce passed two hand grenades in the direction of the American soldiers. Just as the "ting" sound of the grenades bouncing on concrete was heard by at least one soldier, the terrorist reached inside his shirt and detonated his suicide vest.

The initial "grenade" warning and three nearly simultaneous explosions spurred total and immediate chaos. Shrapnel and the dead terrorist's body parts rained down on the area, which only added to the day's already horrendous carnage. All six coalition service members bolted for cover as quickly as possible, but before anyone could blink—let alone check themselves for injuries—each had to somehow get back onto his feet and stay on red alert for more attacks.

That's when someone shouted an ominous and uncertain follow-up warning.

"RED BANDANA!" one of the soldiers screamed at approximately 1602.

Seemingly out of nowhere, a man wearing an ANA uniform who was carrying both an AK-47 and a grenade launcher had jumped out from behind the first set of shipping containers—the side facing the perimeter breach—and started running north. The man in the red bandana then made a virtual arc around the containers before abruptly turning south and sprinting toward the empty water tank, which was behind the six-man patrol.

As soon as Mike heard the warning, his eyes started scanning the area for red. It was only a few seconds before he saw not only the color but the red bandana itself. Through the smoke, Mike soon realized that the terrorist, who he had to assume was wearing a suicide vest like the others, was heading straight toward his Polish counterpart. If Mike didn't immediately confront this imminent threat, the enemy fighter would reach Karol and almost certainly blow himself up.

Instead of moving backward and trying to take cover, Mike raised his M4 carbine rifle and used all of his might to push forward and get between the enemy fighter and Karol while starting to fire. Earl and several other members of the patrol were shooting at the red-bandanaed terrorist as well, but Mike was closest. If the threat was going to be neutralized, he was the soldier best positioned to protect Karol and thus the entire makeshift coalition patrol.

After nearly a decade of training and war fighting, there is little doubt that Mike intrinsically and instinctively knew he was in grave danger as the terrorist in the red bandana charged toward him. There is also little doubt that in the harrowing split-second moment, the thought most likely filling the mind of US Army Staff Sergeant Michael Ollis was saving the life of the Polish soldier he had only just met.

BOOM.

Mike kept his promise to have second lieutenant Karol Cierpica's back. While it's impossible to know if he fired the bullet that hit the insurgent's suicide vest or if it was another member of the patrol, Mike had borne the full brunt of an explosion that occurred only a few seconds after the terrorist in the red bandana was hit by gunfire and fell flat on his face in front of the empty water tank.

The powerful blast occurred only about a yard from where Mike firmly planted his boots on the ground, held his position, and refused to let the suicide bomber reach and almost certainly kill Karol. The force of the explosion was so strong that it flung Mike about ten yards through the air until his back slammed into one of the shipping containers.

Earl had heroic instincts that were similar to Mike's. Upon realizing that a fellow soldier was injured by the explosion, he immediately ran straight toward Mike carrying only a pocketknife to protect himself after having just fired his last two bullets at the man in the red bandana. Earl knew what he had to do: reach the wounded soldier as soon as possible and try to save his life at all costs.

Even though there was still gunfire around them, the moment Earl made it to Mike was strangely quiet. While lying mostly on his back, the top of Mike's shoulders were resting up against the shipping container. Earl could see that he was bleeding, confused, and almost certainly in shock.

As soon as Mike looked up and saw Earl's eyes staring into his, there was one brief moment of calm. It was as if Mike realized he was now in the care of a brother-in-arms and could be at peace. Mike had volunteered to watch Earl's back, and now it was Earl who had his.

Knowing there was no time to spare, Earl began carefully picking Mike up when Karol—who was shouting in Polish—reached them and began trying to help. It took only a few moments for Karol to fall to his knees upon realizing that he had been wounded for a second time during the battle. Even though he wasn't sure exactly which explosion had gashed both of his legs with shrapnel, he knew he could no longer assist Earl in trying to move Mike.

In that painful moment, the Polish soldier fully grasped what his American counterpart had done for him and was emotionally crushed by being physically unable to return the favor.

"Przykro mi!" a tearful Karol shouted to Earl before crawling to safety behind a shipping container and starting to say a prayer for Mike's survival. His emotional words to Earl were Polish for "I'm sorry."

Armed with only that pocketknife, Earl soon located Mike's M4 rifle and checked to see if there was any ammunition. It was empty, which meant that Mike fired all of his thirty bullets at enemy fighters in the minutes between the first explosion and the most recent suicide bombing. Instead of staying safely inside his bunker, Mike had made a conscious choice to run onto the battlefield and go after the enemy with everything he had.

When Earl grabbed Mike by the belt to pick him up, blood came seeping out of the wounded soldier's camouflage pants. After carrying him inside the Copperhead UAV compound, Earl could see that Mike's left arm was badly broken and partially amputated. His right forearm was also shattered. Even worse, Mike had become unresponsive after the initial moment of recognition when Earl first reached him.

Grabbing a now blood-soaked tourniquet that Mike was carrying in his pocket, Earl wrapped it around the injured soldier's arm before using his own tourniquet on one of Mike's severely bleeding legs. Earl then started rubbing Mike's sternum and lightly slapping his face in an effort to elicit some sort of response. Aside from the scattered pops of gunfire that could still be heard outside the UAV compound, there was silence.

Earl then decided to unbutton Mike's camouflage top and rip open his T-shirt to search for other injuries. He was instantly concerned when he saw a deep compression in Mike's chest. What Earl couldn't have known was that the indent was not from the explosion, but the pectus excavatum Mike was born with that had been a constant source of jokes between him and his friends.

Having found what he initially thought was another serious injury, Earl decided that in order to help Mike the most, it was better to stop his first aid efforts and get him to the hospital. It was now 1607—five minutes after the most recent suicide bombing and thirteen after the initial blast.

It was then that Earl ran outside the UAV compound and noticed a civilian contractor who appeared to be American hiding behind one of the shipping containers. Earl then pointed toward a small Gator ATV parked nearby and started shouting.

"Hey, you're safe. Come out from behind that container, go get that Gator and pull it up right here," Earl said. "I've got a badly wounded man inside."

After the contractor pulled up in the small vehicle and helped lay Mike in the back seat, Earl handed him his rifle (even though it had no bullets) and told him to immediately get Mike to the forward surgical team (FST). The only problem was that the contractor didn't know exactly where the hospital was. Earl then rescanned the area and noticed an unknown American soldier.

"You—do you know where the FST is?" Earl shouted. "I need you to get this guy there, now!"

"Yes, sir," said the soldier, who wound up driving Mike to the FST instead of the civilian contractor.

When the US Air Force surgeons, doctors, and nurses began examining Mike inside the FST, he was unresponsive and had already lost a significant amount of blood, which covered not only his uniform pants but also the back seat of the Gator ATV that had brought him there. He had a weak carotid pulse, which meant the situation was critical. After initial efforts to resuscitate failed, the doctors decided to intubate Mike with an endotracheal tube.

FOB Ghazni was still under siege in the late afternoon hours of August 28, 2013, when an announcement came over the emergency-alert loudspeaker. After first being called out in Polish, the ensuing English words shook several soldiers on the base who knew Mike best: Doyle, Eric, Eddie, Shane, Patrick, and all the warriors of Triple Deuce.

"We are in need of O-positive blood to treat a wounded US service member," the voice said. "If your blood type is O-positive and you can safely reach the FST, bring a teammate with you and please promptly report here to the hospital."

No Americans other than Earl and the soldier and contractor who drove him there could have known that the wounded service member was Mike. All they could do was stay inside their respective bunkers, eliminate any ensuing threats, and wait for the battle of FOB Ghazni to finally subside.

"Please don't hurt him, Lord," Bob Ollis prayed in London before even realizing there had been an attack on his son's temporary forward operating base in Afghanistan. "Hurt me."

In eastern Afghanistan, it was wounded Polish army second lieutenant Karol Cierpica who first brought a prayer to the bedside of Bob and Linda's only son. After telling every doctor and nurse who would listen that the critically wounded American had saved his life, Karol begged the Lord to spare Mike's.

The next decision facing the doctors was crucial. The only way to potentially give Mike a new lease on life was to perform a thoracotomy—a complicated procedure that would have used up the base's entire blood supply while fully consuming numerous members of the medical staff. Adding to the uncertainty over whether to perform the procedure was that the success rate of thoracotomy for a patient in Mike's already dire condition was extremely low.

Given that the base was in the middle of a mass-casualty event, with bullets still flying just a few yards from the FST, the surgeons unanimously agreed that a thoracotomy couldn't be performed without depleting their resources and thus endangering the lives of other patients. As the anguished doctors and nurses lowered their heads, it was clear to everybody in the room that the dying warrior's life could no longer be saved.

At 1610—4:10 p.m. local time in Ghazni, Afghanistan—US Army Staff Sergeant Michael Ollis was pronounced dead. He was less than three weeks away from celebrating his twenty-fifth birthday.

As the battle of FOB Ghazni continued for many more hours after Mike's passing, twelve more wounded soldiers and contractors were successfully treated by the FST medical staff. Even in death, Mike's ultimate sacrifice was still saving lives. Based on everything he wrote and is known to have said throughout his relatively short life, forgoing the thoracotomy to give other patients a chance at survival is exactly what Mike would have wanted. The fact that Karol and countless others on the base wound up making it home from Afghanistan only further underscores that Mike's many years of training and dedication to duty had been worth it.

Karol, who had been given morphine as the doctors removed

the shrapnel from his legs, became overwhelmed by grief and guilt upon learning that the American soldier lying next to him had passed away. In that profoundly sad moment, Karol told another US Air Force nurse what had happened on the battlefield only a few minutes earlier.

"That man saved my life," he said in broken English. "Could you please tell me his name?"

"Michael," she said, reading from Mike's dusty dog tag. "His name was Staff Sergeant Michael H. Ollis. He was Roman Catholic."

Covering his face with his blood-soaked hands, Karol spoke directly to the American soldier who shielded him from the suicide-bomb blast. Even though he didn't know much of anything about Mike other than his name and religion, Karol firmly believed that the fallen soldier could hear him from heaven.

"I'm sorry I let you down, Michael," Karol said quietly in Polish. "I will never forget your name or what you did for me today."

Nine excruciating hours later, Private Eric Patterson was still inside the same bunker that Mike had ordered him to defend. He was exhausted, hungry, and badly in need of a trip to the restroom.

"Hey, Leo, I just pissed myself," Eric admitted to Shane as they both started to laugh. "We've gotta get out of this bunker, man."

It wasn't until sometime after 0300 that Eric and Shane finally heard their names called over the emergency-alert loudspeaker. They were then told to report to a nearby rendezvous point. More than eleven hours since the massive first explosion rocked the MWR center and the rest of FOB Ghazni, Eric, Shane, and the others could finally leave the bunker and rejoin the rest of Second Platoon.

"Sergeant Ollie gave the up," Eric said with confidence. "Let's get the hell out of here!"

While being escorted back to their tents by American and

Polish army teams, the soldiers and contractors passed the spot where—unbeknownst to anyone in the group at the time—Mike had made the ultimate sacrifice just over nine hours earlier.

"Don't look at the taxiway," one of the Green Berets told the soldiers and contractors. "Trust me, all of you will want to face forward."

Eric couldn't help himself and looked anyway. What he saw—dozens of body parts, charred debris, bullet holes, and what seemed like buckets of blood that had been dumped all over the shipping containers and even the UAV compound—would stay with him forever. Everyone who even briefly glanced at the taxiway had no doubt that whatever happened there had been catastrophic.

The initial meeting point for Triple Deuce wound up being a basketball court. That's when a lieutenant began counting the soldiers in each squad to make sure everyone was accounted for.

"You're missing one," the lieutenant said while pointing toward Eric and the rest of his squad.

As his heart began to sink, Eric hoped there had been some type of miscommunication.

"Where's Ollis?" Eric asked the platoon sergeant. "He came to give you an up."

"He never came here, Private," the platoon sergeant said.

Eric, Shane, and the other soldiers in his squad immediately started running over to their tents, where they hoped to find Mike relaxing inside of his. Every tent was empty. That's when Doyle came up to them.

"Did Ollie make it back here?" asked Doyle, who was deeply afraid of getting the wrong answer.

"No," someone said. "And the platoon sergeant just said he wants to see all of us."

By this point, Eric was almost positive that something had happened to Mike, who wouldn't have simply disappeared almost ten full hours after leaving the bunker. By that point, Eric could only pray that Mike had suffered some sort of injury and would survive. Those hopes began to fade when Eric and the others saw a captain and a major walk into the tent where the soldiers of Triple Deuce had gathered in a circle for the platoon sergeant's announcement.

While everyone else was still waiting in the tent, the platoon sergeant told the squad leaders to take a seat.

"We have one confirmed KIA," he said. "It's Staff Sergeant Ollis."

"Are you serious?" said Doyle, who suddenly felt like the entire world had started crashing down around him.

"Yes," the platoon sergeant said. "I'm sorry. We are still trying to figure out exactly what happened. He might have been hit by a mortar or maybe even one of the suicide bombers."

"That kid can't die," Doyle said as he tripped on a bedpost and fell backward. "It's not who he is."

Doyle was holding back tears when he walked into the tent with the other squad leader and platoon sergeant. He knew the news would devastate Second Platoon and the entire Tenth Mountain Division, which hadn't suffered a single combat death so far during their 2013 Afghanistan deployment. Doyle also knew someone would have to tell Schnell, who was still at Bagram Airfield.

The captain wound up making the announcement, which left most of the soldiers in utter disbelief.

"He's going to be okay, right?" said Eric, whose mind couldn't comprehend the news.

"Did you not hear the captain?" the soldier next to Eric said. "Ollis is KIA. That means he's dead."

When it finally dawned on Eric that Mike was gone, he picked up his helmet and flung it across the tent. Eric then jumped onto a bunk bed and began to sob.

"I'm the reason he's gone," Eric told a teammate who was trying to console him. "I didn't fight hard enough and get him to stay inside that bunker."

Eddie, Patrick, and Shane also tried to comfort Eric, who would blame himself for Mike's death for several years before ultimately realizing that it wasn't his fault. Eric was only eighteen when his squad leader was killed, but was forced to grapple with raw and difficult emotions experienced by thousands of combat veterans who have returned home from the battlefield without a brother- or sister-in-arms.

At Bagram Airfield, Schnell was woken up and greeted with a choppy phone call full of static. After being told there had been a major enemy assault on FOB Ghazni, the platoon sergeant informed him that someone was killed in action.

"It's Mike," he said.

"Who is Mike?" said the tired and confused squad leader, who was used to referring to everyone by his last name or—in Mike's case—his A-Team nickname.

"Ollis, man, Mike Ollis," the platoon sergeant said. "I'm so sorry."

After hanging up the phone, speaking with a chaplain, and consoling a group of soldiers who knew Mike, Schnell went outside and began to punch a concrete divider on the large base.

"Why, God?" he yelled. "Why did it have to be Ollis?"

Mike's death—while tragic—was not in vain. The Taliban's August 28, 2013, attack on FOB Ghazni was bold and dramatic, but it would nevertheless become known as a complete failure that caused them to abandon plans to stage similar attacks on other coalition bases. Thanks to the courage of soldiers like Mike, Staff Sergeant Earl Plumlee, their American teammates, and countless Polish and Afghan soldiers, the base remained in coalition hands once the smoke cleared. All ten Taliban fighters who penetrated the base were dead, along with scores of additional insurgents outside the perimeter.

One Polish soldier was shot in the head and killed in the

firefight's opening minutes. Dozens more soldiers were injured, including US, Polish, and Afghan troops. Mike was the only American to make the ultimate sacrifice during the battle of Forward Operating Base Ghazni on August 28, 2013.

As it turned out, Karol wasn't the only person in danger outside the Copperhead UAV compound who survived because of Mike. While subsequently being interviewed by military investigators, the contractor who Earl had first noticed hiding behind a shipping container revealed that because of Mike's willingness to courageously confront and neutralize the suicide bomber, many more American civilian workers were able to escape the area.

"When you consider the degree of what was happening inside our compound, even before alarms had gone off, the fact that Staff Sergeant Ollis came and defended us and we were a bunch of unarmed civilians means everything to me," said the contractor, whose name is redacted in the official US Army investigative report. "It was a tough situation to be in and body parts were flying everywhere, and he helped protect us."

"I've got nothing but gratitude and respect for Staff Sergeant Ollis," the contractor continued. "It looked like we were targeted and it is amazing that no one in our compound was killed. He gave his life helping to protect over forty unarmed civilians."

"Dad, I just got a call from your next-door neighbor on Burbank Avenue," said Mike's oldest sister Kim, who was calling her parents in England from central New Jersey. "I don't want you to get nervous, but there's a military vehicle sitting outside your house with two soldiers inside."

"Did Tom [the neighbor] say what they look like?" Bob said. "What are they wearing?"

"They're younger guys," said Kim. "I believe Tom said they're wearing dress uniforms."

This is not good, Bob thought.

Kim, who was standing on the sidelines at a soccer field watching her son's game, then explained that the uniformed soldiers wouldn't release any information to the neighbor, who had told them that Bob and Linda were on vacation in Europe. Tom then gave them Kim's number, which the soldiers promptly called. Despite her pleas, the soldiers gently refused to provide Kim with more information other than giving her a phone number for Bob and Linda to call.

As a combat veteran himself, Bob knew the situation was potentially serious. After hanging up with Kim, Bob and Linda briefly discussed what was now the best-case scenario in an unimaginably awful situation.

"Maybe he's been wounded," Linda said to Bob while trying to keep her composure.

"That would mean they're flying Michael to Germany," Bob said. "If that's the case, at least we're not far from him."

As Linda began to pack her suitcase, Bob called the phone number that the soldiers had given to Kim. On the other end of the line was a US Army sergeant who said he was stationed at Fort Dix, an army-support-activity center at Joint Base McGuire-Dix-Lakehurst in the southern half of New Jersey.

When Bob politely asked what was going on, the sergeant explained that he was under strict orders not to divulge any details over the phone. Instead, the sergeant said, Bob and Linda should expect a visit from two US Army soldiers at 0700 local time at their London hotel room. After thanking the sergeant, Bob hung up the phone and said a quick prayer.

"Please don't hurt him, Lord," he whispered as Big Ben struck 1 a.m. in London. "Hurt me."

Upon realizing that they would have to wait six agonizing hours to find out what happened to their son, Bob and Linda decided to get some air. As they walked through the quiet streets of London in the middle of the night, the worried parents couldn't have known that at that very moment, their son lay draped in dignity by an American flag as preparations were being made to fly his body to Bagram Airfield.

There, Schnell and others were waiting to mourn and pay tribute to their fallen friend before he was flown back to American soil, where Mike's loved ones would—even though they didn't know it yet—be waiting to receive his remains at Dover Air Force Base in Delaware.

As the painful US-military-casualty notification process began in earnest, an emotionally crushed Staff Sergeant Doyle Davis sat down inside his tent to write a letter to the soon-to-be grieving family of his friend and fellow soldier:

> *I am not sure how the bonds in our line of work are formed. I am sure that there is some kind of psychological or scientific explanation to it, but within days of assuming his duties as a squad leader, "Ollie" became one of the good ole boys. It was like he was always there and took his rightful place in the platoon. Almost immediately, he was in the platoon office arguing with Schnell and me over who should give up guys for what detail and who deserved to go to the next available Army school. It was during those heated discussions that we all hated that we found the love we had for one another. We all understood that we only fought with each other so passionately because we cared for our respective men and loved each other as brothers.*
>
> *Ollis applied the same dedication to his off time that he did to his duties at work. His strength of character positively impacted the life of every man who had the privilege of knowing Ollis on a personal level. Regardless of the numerous nicknames we bestowed upon him, I knew him above all as my friend. If "Ollie" was nothing else, he was a fierce, fierce friend.*

I could probably go on for ages about how much Michael meant to me, but I will leave this final word. I weep not for the one who has gone, but for those of us left behind trying to pick up the pieces of our shattered hearts. For a light that once shone in this dark lonely world, a beacon to lead us to better shores has extinguished far too soon, leaving us adrift in a sea of most beloved memories.

In the coming days, the ultimate sacrifice made by US Army Staff Sergeant Michael Ollis at Forward Operating Base Ghazni would reverberate through not only Staten Island and numerous parts of the United States but also an entire European country that would soon learn of his final heroic deed.

CHAPTER 13

DEEDS NOT WORDS

M r. and Mrs. Ollis, the secretary of the army and the president of the United States have entrusted me to express their deep regret that your son, Staff Sergeant Michael Harold Ollis, was killed in action in the Ghazni Province of Afghanistan on August 28, 2013, while conducting combat operations," a US Army casualty assistance officer (CAO) told Bob and Linda. "The secretary and the president extend their deepest sympathy to you and your family in your loss."

While hugging and consoling his devastated wife, Bob—just before his mind and body went almost entirely numb—first focused on three words: "killed in action." To the Vietnam War veteran, those words indicated that his son had gone down fighting. Without knowing a single detail of what Michael had done at FOB Ghazni that day, the only emotion stronger than sadness was the immense pride Bob felt for his son.

"Your son died a hero," the CACO said inside their London hotel room.

Linda and Bob then started placing tearful phone calls to family members back home and had incredibly painful and difficult conversations with Kim and Kelly. Nothing can prepare a parent for having to tell their children about the death of a sibling, especially over the phone while separated by an ocean.

In New Jersey, Kim and Bill then had to tell William and Joseph that their beloved Uncle Mike wasn't coming home alive from Afghanistan. Thomas was too young to understand, as were Kelly and Dave's children, Ava and Matthew, whom they were raising in Maryland.

That evening in London, Bob and Linda were whisked through security at Heathrow Airport to board a flight bound for Philadelphia. They were treated like royalty by the British Airways flight attendants, who sat them in first class and constantly came over to check on them. The pilot even came out of the cockpit while Linda happened to be sleeping to extend his condolences to Bob.

Upon landing in Philadelphia, Bob and Linda were greeted by a staff member from the USO. She assured America's newest Gold Star parents that they would be fully taken care of while awaiting the arrival of family members and, of course, Michael, whose coffin would be draped in an American flag as he was carried off a US Air Force C-17 aircraft at Dover Air Force Base. The dignified transfer ceremony was originally planned for August 30 but was subsequently delayed to the next day due to mechanical issues with the C-17.

Mike's parents were then driven from Philadelphia to Delaware, where they would stay at Dover Air Force Base's Fisher House, which was specially built by the eponymous charity organization for families of the fallen. During the short trip, the US Army soldier sitting in the passenger's seat—an NCO like Mike—turned around to speak to Bob and Linda. The Gold Star parents could tell he had something important to say.

"You know that your son was a hero, right?" he said before an awkward moment of silence. Bob and Linda were still numb with grief and didn't know what to say at first.

"The CACO told us something similar over in London, but

we haven't gotten any details yet about what Michael did," Bob said.

"I can't imagine how hard this is for both of you," the NCO said. "You'll be given a more detailed briefing soon, but from what I've been told, a Polish army officer is alive right now because of your son. Michael shielded him from an explosion."

"Did this happen on the base he had just gotten to—FOB Ghazni?" Bob asked.

"I believe so, yes, sir," the NCO said.

"Thank you, Sergeant," Bob said while patting the NCO on the shoulder.

"Father God, as we gather here today to remember Staff Sergeant Michael Ollis, we ask that you bless and comfort us as we grieve this untimely loss," a US Army chaplain said. "Be gracious to his family, his friends, his platoon, his company, and his fellow soldiers here today. We thank you God for the life, service, and sacrifice of Staff Sergeant Ollis: our brother and friend. It is our privilege to have served with him."

Inside a chapel on America's largest base in Afghanistan, more than two hundred deployed American warfighters gathered to honor Mike. Beneath the podium at the base of the chapel's altar stood the battlefield cross, which consisted of Mike's helmet, rifle, dog tags, boots, and newest medals resting on a black platform. Those medals were the Bronze Star—identical to the medal Mike proudly pinned on his father's chest just over four years earlier—and the Purple Heart. His buddies also added two cans of Snapple to the display while fondly remembering how happy the drink had made him when their platoon had first arrived at FOB Warrior.

For many soldiers in the room—especially those from the Bushmaster 2–22nd Infantry Regiment—Triple Deuce—it was the most emotional moment of their Afghanistan deployment and one of the saddest days of their lives. Mike's body had been escorted from FOB Ghazni to Bagram the night before by Shane and another soldier, Seamus Redmond, who were met by Schnell at the helicopter landing pad to carry their fallen teammate's body off of the UH-60 Black Hawk. In a letter he later sent to Bob and Linda, Seamus—who lovingly referred to Mike's parents as "mom and dad"—wrote that "I'm very honored to have served with your son who I call my brother. Not a day goes by that I don't wish I was by his side fighting. I know he would have chewed me out later for not listening to him, but I would have at least done something with him.

"I know my wife is very grateful that I'm home and alive," Seamus wrote in closing. "[Mike] did save a lot of lives that day. I won't ever forget him and I know you two miss him dearly. He is our Tiny Ranger hero—always leading the way."

Sitting front and center at the Bagram Airfield memorial was US Army Major General James McConville, who was not only the commander of Mike's former 101st Airborne Division, but the entire Regional Command East mission in Afghanistan. The general appeared stoic yet emotional at times. Throughout the ceremony, it was clear that the events of August 28, 2013, and the loss of a soldier under his command were deeply affecting the general.

During the ceremony, the commander of Triple Deuce—US Army Colonel Brett Funck—spoke about a meeting he had with Mike in his office just before Mike left for Ranger School: "He said, 'Sir, you have nothing to worry about with me. They're not gonna kick me out of there; they're not gonna get me out of there. I'm coming home Ranger-qualified—whatever happens and however long it takes me,'" Colonel (now Brigadier General) Funck shared. He added, "And we all know the rest of the story— Sergeant Ollis came back a few months later with everyone else I spoke with amongst that group and everyone else was Ranger-qualified, too.

"The point I want to talk about here is that I honestly believe that Sergeant Ollis possessed an infectious type of positive leadership that really drove others around him to excel," the colonel continued. "He was one of those leaders you looked at and had a lot of energy. I always saw a smile on his face, and it always made me proud to be with him."

Colonel Funck, who said Mike embodied Sergeant Audie Murphy's call to "lead from the front," then closed his remarks by reciting part of the US Army Ranger creed, before saying "Deeds not words"—Triple Deuce's official motto.

US Army Captain William McMurray, the commander of Bushmaster Company, spoke next.

"During the first week of August, the Sergeant Audie Murphy Club selected Staff Sergeant Ollis as the most recent inductee representing the First Brigade of the Tenth Mountain Division," Captain McMurray said. "Staff Sergeant Ollis continuously demonstrated his hunger for knowledge. He was equally dedicated to imparting this knowledge to develop men by coaching, training, and mentoring.

"Staff Sergeant Ollis undoubtedly woke up every morning to take care of his soldiers," the captain said later in his speech. "His personality was that of a big brother: always taking the time to care for his baby brothers. He always fought for his men."

To anyone in the room who knew Staff Sergeant Ollis, the third and final speaker needed no introduction because he could almost always be found at Mike's side. After taking a deep breath, Staff Sergeant Brian Schnell began eulogizing his fellow squad leader and dear friend:

> Staff Sergeant Michael Ollis had many nicknames. Most of them I gave to him—Mighty Mouse, Tiny Ranger, Ollie Murphy—but above all, I knew him as a friend. We never used first names when addressing each other even though we were so close. I guess when you grow up in the army

at such a young age like we did, it's just more natural to use last names, even when we were just hanging out.

I first met him in 2011 when he was assigned to my squad. The first thing we did together was a six-mile ruck march. I first noticed something about Ollis: even though he was just coming off PCS leave from Fort Campbell, it was the fact that he didn't give up. I probably had the longest stride in the platoon, and he could have just quit and fallen back, but he didn't. The faster I went, there he was right alongside me. I said, "Are you doing okay Ollis?" [mispronouncing Mike's last name as OH-lis]. His only response was "It's AH-lis. My name is Ollis, Sergeant."

As the months went by, he proved to be the most aggressive teammate I've ever had in the army. I finally had my bulldog, so I didn't need to be one anymore. Soon, all the squad leaders got together to discuss who will fill the position of First Squad leader. There was no argument, for once. It would be Ollis. Within a week, Ollis went to the promotion board for staff sergeant and knocked it out of the park.

Now he was my peer, and our friendship grew. He was a perfect fit for an awesome corps of squad leaders. We were so close that we called ourselves the "A-Team." Mac: Hannibal, Davis: Murdock, Me: BA, and Ollis: Face. We would all hum the theme song, which was way better than hearing Davis sing.

Ollis and I were so competitive with each other. I always wanted to beat him at running and he always wanted to [challenge] me in the gym. His favorite thing to punish me after a workout was to run Sackets Harbor—all of Sackets Harbor, battlefield and all. "Come on, Big Dummy, I'll race you." Afterwards, we'd go to the brewery, have lunch, and maybe catch a Jets game.

He loved the kids in our group. After Melissa had Maddie and Ollis got back from Ranger School, he'd come over to my place and play with my daughter. It seemed like that was all the entertainment we needed. He was just fascinated by her. There was a softer side to Ollis that not many saw.

I remember the last weekend when we were at home; his dad came up. It was great to sit and talk with the man who Ollis spoke so highly of.

[Our training at Fort Drum] ended with both of us saying "It's you and me, brother. I wouldn't want to do it with anyone else." I don't think my wife, who also loved Ollis very much, got the bond that two men have especially when they're about to go to war. This was both of our third deployment. We used to say "third time's a charm."

Ollis was a great leader. He was motivated and a hard charger, but what made him truly great was that he loved his guys. He fought for them every chance he got. He strived to always make things better for his men. He was a fighter—everyone knows that. We clashed on many, many subjects, and I'm sure all of you are very shocked by that statement, but we fought—a lot. I mean a lot. But afterwards, we would always laugh and I'd let him down from one of the lockers, and then he'd hit me one more time.

A couple days ago, Davis said "I could see him up there arguing with St. Peter to let one more person in." Well, I hope that if I get to go to heaven—I know that's where he is—I hope to see my friend Ollis at the pearly gates. That he fights to get me in, just so he can call me "Big Dummy." I'm glad to have been so fortunate to know Ollis the man. I have many memories, all of which will last me a lifetime.

Ollis: I know you're listening and saying "Schnell, end this speech already, Big Dummy." So I'm going to end it like this. Hey Tiny Ranger: I miss you. I can't wait for all the members of the A-Team to be together again. There are no goodbyes for us, only "see you laters." So I'll see ya, man, in the next life.

"Company: Attention!" the first sergeant roared shortly after Schnell concluded his emotional speech. "Specialist Marshall!"

"Here, First Sergeant!" the first soldier shouted in response.

"Corporal McTighe!" the first sergeant said.

"Here, First Sergeant!" Patrick said.

"Staff Sergeant Ollis!" the first sergeant yelled.

"Staff Sergeant Michael Ollis!

"Staff Sergeant Michael H. Ollis!"

As every soldier stood at attention, the total silence in the room was then broken by a twenty-one-gun salute being fired outside at Bagram Airfield to honor the Tenth Mountain Division's newest fallen hero.

BOOM. BOOM. BOOM.

After "Taps," the sounds of bagpipes filled the chapel as "Amazing Grace" was played. Mike's commanding officers knelt before the battlefield cross, said a prayer, and left commemorative coins that would eventually be given to Bob and Linda. Then, it was time for the soldiers of Triple Deuce to do the same in what was the most poignant and personal moment of the entire ceremony.

"He was a great role model," an emotional Corporal Eddie Garcia said in a short video recorded in front of Mike's battlefield cross. "He taught me a lot."

General James McConville then slowly saluted Staff Sergeant Michael Ollis before kneeling before the battlefield cross and saying a prayer. He would spend the ensuing weeks, months, and years ensuring that Mike's ultimate sacrifice was appropriately recognized and that his family always had everything they needed.

"Thro' many dangers, toils and snares, I have already come,"

John Newton's "Amazing Grace" poem goes. "'Tis grace hath brought me safe thus far, and grace will lead me home."

After being carried onto a huge military jet by Schnell, Shane, and Seamus and being slowly saluted one last time by his grieving fellow soldiers in Afghanistan, it was time for Staff Sergeant Michael Ollis to come home.

August 31, 2013, was a warm and beautiful day in Delaware. It was a Saturday—the start of Labor Day weekend—and the skies above Dover Air Force Base were bright, blue, and clear.

For two American families, the day became cold and dark when a massive US Air Force C-17 Globemaster III military transport aircraft first appeared in the sky. It was carrying the flag-draped caskets of two fallen US Army soldiers who made the ultimate sacrifice in Afghanistan's Ghazni Province: Staff Sergeant Michael Ollis and Sergeant First Class Ricardo Young.

Sergeant First Class Young, a thirty-four-year-old Arkansas native who was married with two children, was killed in a different August 28, 2013, battle while leading his patrol up a mountain. For his heroism, Sergeant First Class Young would soon—like Mike—posthumously receive the Silver Star.

Just before the C-17 made its approach, the Young and Ollis families boarded a bus that would take them from the Fisher House to one of Dover Air Force Base's runways. One by one, the Youngs and Bob, Linda, Kim, Bill, Kelly, and Dave stepped off the bus and were led by their respective casualty assistance officers and chaplains toward a row of chairs, where several US military dignitaries were waiting to greet them and offer their condolences.

Only a Gold Star family member can know what it feels like to see their son, daughter, husband, wife, brother, or sister return from a war zone in a coffin covered by an American flag. A dignified transfer is perhaps the most sacred ceremony in the entire US military, with hundreds of service members and volunteers working in unison to ensure that a fallen hero's remains and grieving relatives are treated with the utmost reverence and respect.

Just like his commanding officers and teammates in Afghanistan, many service members saluted Mike as his casket was carried off the C-17. On that sad day in Dover, however, one salute meant the most. It was from Bob Ollis, who had narrowly survived one war only to see his son killed in another more than four decades later. Throughout his life, Mike's mission was to honor his father's service and make him proud. Bob would now do the same for his only son.

I wish I could have been there to help you, Bob thought as he first laid eyes on his son's casket. All he wanted to do was to give Michael a hug, no matter what condition his body was in. Bob then suddenly became frustrated that he wasn't even allowed to touch the coffin during the ceremony. As seven soldiers slowly carried the casket by the row of chairs, Bob reached out with one hand and tried. Sadly, he was too far away. After lowering his head in grief, Bob hugged his wife and daughters.

For Linda, the day's events at Dover were so surreal that she felt like she was in a movie. In fact, she had recently watched *Taking Chance,* a 2009 HBO film starring Kevin Bacon that painstakingly portrays the dignified transfer and military funeral process. As she boarded the bus back to the Fisher House, the Gold Star mom thought about the fallen marine for whom the movie was named: US Marine Lance Corporal Chance Phelps, who was killed in Iraq nine years before her son's death in Afghanistan. Linda also thought about and prayed for the thousands of other American families who had been through the same tragic experience at Dover in the nearly twelve years since her city was attacked on 9/11.

In a fateful yet fitting coincidence, US Army Staff Sergeant Michael Ollis would return to his home state on a day that meant so much to the soldier and his fellow New Yorkers: September

11. On the twelfth anniversary of the worst terrorist attack in the city and nation's history, a fallen hometown hero would return to Staten Island after making the ultimate sacrifice in the country where the atrocities were planned. American forces had killed Osama bin Laden more than two years earlier, but as Mike's death underscored, the war in Afghanistan was far from over.

From Afghanistan, General McConville wrote a letter to Bob and Linda that arrived while they were preparing for their son's September 14, 2013, funeral, which would take place in Staten Island with full military honors:

> *Dear Mrs. and Mrs. Ollis,*
> *On behalf of every member of Combined Joint Task Force—101 and Regional Command East, Afghanistan, please accept my most sincere condolences for the loss of your son, Staff Sergeant Michael H. Ollis.*
>
> *Michael rendered the ultimate sacrifice in defense of our nation and the people of Afghanistan with true bravery and intrepidity in the face of enemy fire and was directly responsible for saving the lives of other soldiers at his forward operating base. His actions directly contributed to the success of our mission to advise and assist the Afghan National Security Forces as they secure their country and ensured the safety of his fellow soldiers.*
>
> *Michael will forever be honored amongst those few true heroes of our nation. He will forever be remembered as a Screaming Eagle, a warrior, a brother in arms and a true friend to all who knew him.*
>
> > *Sincerely,*
> > *James C. McConville*
> > *Major General, US Army*
> > *Commanding*

A similar letter to Bob and Linda soon arrived from US Army Lieutenant General Mark Milley, who was then the commander of the International Security Assistance Force Joint Command in Kabul, Afghanistan. General Milley, who would become chairman of the Joint Chiefs of Staff a few years later, added a handwritten note that said "All of our thoughts and prayers are with you and your family." General Lloyd Austin, then the commander of US Central Command who would later become secretary of defense, also sent a letter of condolence.

Then secretary of defense Chuck Hagel—like Bob, a wounded veteran who volunteered to serve in Vietnam—mailed a letter to the Gold Star family as well:

> Dear Mr. and Mrs. Ollis,
> I realize words provide little comfort or solace, but I want to offer you and your family my deepest sympathy and personal condolences during this most difficult time. Our men and women in uniform voluntarily make extraordinary sacrifices in their service to our nation, and your son made the ultimate sacrifice. I know his loss leaves an enormous void in your lives.
> At this critical time in our history, Staff Sergeant Michael Ollis answered the call to duty and served a cause bigger than himself in Afghanistan. A grateful nation will never forget his willingness to uphold the values that make America unique in human history.
>   With my deepest sympathy, sincerely,
>   Chuck Hagel

"God bless you," the defense secretary added in blue marker.

Mike's final act of heroism clearly made an impression on military leaders. Almost immediately, he was nominated for the nation's third-highest military honor, the Silver Star, which would be swiftly approved and become official that October. An early draft of the Silver Star citation left no doubt that Mike died while saving Karol and many others:

> For conspicuous gallantry and intrepidity under fire on 28 August 2013 while assigned to Bravo Company, 2nd Battalion, 22nd Infantry Regiment, in support of Operation Enduring Freedom. Staff Sergeant Ollis' actions during a complex enemy attack against FOB Ghazni directly prevented armed insurgents from gaining access to the populated areas of FOB Ghazni after they breached the outer wall.
>
> Staff Sergeant Ollis personally shielded a wounded Polish officer from enemy fire, potentially saving his life, and by interdicting the enemy, saved the lives of numerous coalition soldiers and civilians. Staff Sergeant Ollis' actions are in keeping with the finest traditions of military service and reflect great credit upon himself; 2nd Battalion, 22nd Infantry Regiment; 1st Brigade Combat Team, 10th Mountain Division; Combined Joint Task Force 101, and the United States Army.

A letter from a Polish army general to Bob and Linda confirmed that indeed, a foreign soldier had survived the attack on FOB Ghazni because of Mike:

> *Dear Parents [with a handwritten "Dear Linda! Dear Robert!"],*
> *At the beginning of my letter I would like to introduce myself. I was the Commander of the XIII rotation of the Polish military contingent in Afghanistan. I was the leader*

*during this furious and deceptive terrorist attack on the
Ghazni base. I was the witness of your son's act of valor,
standing 50 meters from the scene.*

*The service, together with your son during the XIII
rotation was the highest honor for me. Covering [another]
soldier with [your] own body is the highest act of sacrificing
and moral triumph over the enemy. Every one of us soldiers
learn it during military service. However, only Michael
showed what [it] in fact means to be a great soldier, saving
[another] soldier. He showed to all of us how wonderful [a]
man he has been and will always be in our hearts. His act
of valor and his short 24-year life is a model to follow for
all soldiers.*

*His death was not in vain. Michael gave away what
he had most valuable, his life, for saving my Polish friend,
my subordinate, sub-lieutenant, but also for the freedom
and democracy for which we were fighting there. We all will
remember him and his act of valor!*

*Please accept my thanks. Thank you, dear parents, that
you brought up Michael and were such a good example to
follow for him. Please [give] my compliments also to the
sisters of Staff Sergeant Michael H. Ollis.*

> *Glory of the Heroes! Sincerely,*
> *Brigadier General Marek Sokolowski*
> *16 Mechanized Division*
> *Deputy Commander—Chief of Staff*

Political leaders from both New York and the national stage also
began sending condolence letters to the Ollis family. In addition
to Governor Andrew Cuomo and Mayor Michael Bloomberg,
Bob and Linda received a letter from Senator Chuck Schumer,
who would later become the majority leader of the US Senate:

To the parents of Staff Sergeant Michael Ollis:
Words cannot express the grief that I share in learning of
Michael's death. As a New Yorker my heart is heavy with
sorrow with the news that a soldier from New York has lost
his life serving his country valiantly. Though I cannot begin
to know the emotions you are feeling, my prayers are with
you, and your friends and your family during this very
difficult time.

Please accept my deepest condolences and heartfelt
sympathies on your tremendous loss. Michael was a patriot
who bravely answered his nation's call and made the ultimate sacrifice in service of this great country.

I know it is difficult to lose a loved one, especially your
beloved son; but I hope you will take comfort in knowing
the fond memories you share of Michael's spirit, dedication,
courage, strength of character, and love of country, will live
on in you, your family and in the hearts and minds of those
who knew and loved him dearly.

If I can ever be of service to you and your family, please
do not hesitate to call me directly at [phone number].

Sincerely,
Charles E. Schumer
United States Senator

Mike's parents also received a signed condolence letter and
certificate of recognition from the forty-fourth president of the
United States:

Dear Linda and Robert:
I am deeply saddened by the loss of your son, Staff Sergeant Michael H. Ollis, USA. Our nation will not forget
his sacrifice, and we can never repay our debt to your family.

A simple letter cannot ease the pain of losing a child,
but I hope you take solace in knowing that his brave service
exceeded all measures of selflessness and devotion to this
country. We honor him not only as a guardian of our liberty,
but also as the true embodiment of America's spirit of ser-
vice to a cause greater than ourselves.

Michelle and I offer our heartfelt sympathy, and pray
that God's grace gives you comfort as you grieve. In life,
your son was a shining example of all that is best in our
land. In rest, may he find the peace we all seek.

Sincerely,
Barack Obama

While Bob and Linda were extremely grateful to receive condolence letters and phone calls from so many political and military leaders, nothing meant more than hearing from those who knew and cared for their son. One was from Wendy Petersen, a site manager at FOB Ghazni for AirScan, a private military contractor.

"[Mike] selflessly jumped into the fight and directly prevented what could have been catastrophic casualties," she wrote. "I know at least forty of the civilians on our compound that day directly attribute their safety and lives to your son."

"We have re-named our compound 'Camp Ollis' in his memory and we will never forget the sacrifice he made to save countless lives," Wendy wrote a few paragraphs later. "The flag accompanying this letter was flown over the FOB during the dedication ceremony that we conducted in conjunction with the Polish contingent."

Wendy's letter then lists every leg of the long journey to deliver the flag: from FOB Ghazni to Bagram Airfield, Afghanistan to the United Arab Emirates, Dubai to Austria, and Vienna to John F. Kennedy International Airport in New York. The letter lists the names of thirty-six military and civilian pilots and crew members who participated in making sure the American flag, which was flown "in the esteemed position, ahead of everyone, in the windshields of each aircraft," according to Wendy's letter, safely arrived in Staten Island all the way from the mountains of eastern Afghanistan.

Another condolence letter arrived from Melissa Schnell, whose husband was still serving with the rest of Triple Deuce on FOB Shank, where Mike would have also been stationed if he had survived the attack on FOB Ghazni.

"I have in my possession a tough box of Michael's that my husband had sent to our house for him," she wrote. "Brian would like to deliver it to you in person after he arrives home from Afghanistan. He is due to return in October."

Melissa then began sharing some fond memories of Mike:

> [Brian] actually told me that he used to joke with Mike that he spent more time lying next to him than me, which might actually be true at this point. From the little time I knew Mike, it was easy to see he was a real genuine guy. He always found a way to smile no matter what the situation. He seemed to just fit in with everyone.
>
> I'll never forget how much he loved to talk to our infant daughter, Madeline, it was always "hey there, beautiful!" when he saw her. He sure must have loved being with his nephews and niece when he could.
>
> Mike was one of the guys I know Brian had a lot of respect for. I know this because Brian actually listened to him and took his advice—yes, it's a big deal. Those two had a great friendship going on, I know they had made quite a few plans for the upcoming year. I have to say that I was getting just as excited for Michael to come home as I was for Brian.
>
> Once again, I would like to say I am so sorry for your

*loss. I pray that you are all able to find comfort in each
other and comfort in knowing Michael is now able to watch
over his men and his family from a much better place.*

Sincerely,
Melissa Schnell

Kim received an email from a platoon leader who served with
Mike:

Mrs. Loschiavo,

*My uncle had mentioned that you were a teacher at his
daughter's school. I did know Michael and we worked together from the time I first came down to Bravo Company
all the way through the deployment.*

*Michael was in 2nd Platoon and I was the platoon
leader for 3rd Platoon. Our platoons worked side-by-side
throughout the train-up and through the deployment. We
spent the beginning of our deployment together at COP
[Muqur] and relocated to FOB Ghazni as a company. He
was an incredible man and an even more impressive soldier
and NCO. He was an incredible leader and the respect and
devotion he gained from his squad was amazing.*

*I don't think there was a more tight-knit squad in either
of our platoons and it was clear why. Staff Sergeant Ollis
was the true embodiment of what a leader should be and I
am a truly better leader, a better officer, and a better person for
knowing him.*

Sincerely,
Jason Grube

Soldiers from Mike's previous combat tours also began to
reach out to the Ollis family. Those grieving veterans included

Roy Patterson, one of the "Renegades" who served with Mike in Kandahar on his first Afghanistan deployment:

To the family of Staff Sergeant Mike H. Ollis,

Your loss is my loss, your pain is mine as well. I served with your son at Fort Campbell, Kentucky. I deployed with him to Afghanistan in 2010.

Staff Sergeant Ollis was my team leader while we served together. He was my mentor. Your son made a huge impact on my life and my military career. Mike taught me everything I know about being an infantry soldier and non-commissioned officer.

Everywhere Mike went he was loved. He was strict and tough, having a commanding presence and at the same time fair and willing to cut a joke with the team. I always strived to be like him—in Afghanistan he had bandanas he wore under his helmet, so I asked him for one so I could be like him. He was a fearless fighter, so I became fearless too.

I'm writing this letter to let you know your son meant a lot to a lot of people. I was going to come up to New York to see him when he got home, and I'm saddened that it won't happen.

I'm not sure I'll ever get over his death. The world is so much darker now that he's gone. I've spent most days since August 28 praying for a deployment; I'm angry and I want revenge. Mike and our team lost a lot of guys on that deployment and now him—it doesn't seem fair.

If there is anything your family needs through this rough time, let me know.

My utmost condolences,
Sergeant Roy Patterson—"Patty"

Countless more soldiers and Afghanistan and Iraq War veterans were crushed by the news of Mike's death, including close friends like Brian Constantino and Jason Matney, both of whom flew to New York to mourn and serve as pallbearers in their friend and fellow soldier's military funeral.

After receiving confirmation that Mike had been killed in action and that his family had been formally notified, an anguished Tino placed his first phone call to Rob, who was vacationing with Mike's other closest childhood friends in Hilton Head. For Rob, Jimmy, Alanna, Kristen, and Quaseem, the drive from palm tree–lined coastal South Carolina back to the skyscrapers of New York was the longest and most painful trip of their lives.

Tino spoke to Jason next to coordinate their travel plans before then calling someone he knew was deeply important to Mike: Courtney. As she grieved the death of a young man she loved so much, all Courtney could think about was her final conversation with Mike. It was in FOB Ghazni's MWR when Mike told her that he "can't wait to get home and start the rest of my life."

Courtney was overwhelmed with heartache that Mike wouldn't have a chance to get married and raise children someday, even if it wasn't ultimately with her. She knew he would have made a great husband and father. The news also shocked Courtney's parents:

Dear Mr. and Mrs. Ollis, Kelly, Kim and Family:
We offer our sincerest sympathy to you all in the loss of
your son and brother, Michael. During the four or five times
he visited our home with our daughter, Courtney, we came
to love him.

We will keep Michael safely in our hearts. We will
remember his smiling face, his contagious laugh, his drive to
succeed, his gentle demeanor and the love he exuded for his
family, friends and country. We will speak of him often and
remember him always.

We were certainly heartbroken but certainly not sur-
prised to hear of his selfless act that saved others. We are so
proud of Michael.

There is a song from the Broadway musical "Wicked"
titled "For Good." The lyrics remind us so much of
Michael's life and what he meant to Courtney and us. It
begins, "I've heard it said, that people come into our lives
for a reason."

God bless you and your family and God bless Michael:
a man among men.

> *Deepest sympathy,*
> *Robert and Twila*

Marissa, Katherine, and presumably every other young woman who had romantic relationships with Mike shared in Courtney's profound sense of sadness and grief. While he never got the chance to marry or even get engaged, Mike made a point to treat the women in his life with thoughtfulness and respect.

As Courtney, Tino, Jason, and many other friends and relatives began traveling from around the country to join fellow mourners in Staten Island, it was time for Mike's flag-draped casket to be driven north from Dover Air Force Base in Delaware to the Hanley Funeral Home on New Dorp Lane in Staten Island. As bells tolled at Ground Zero in lower Manhattan, where the names of all 9/11 victims were being read on the twelfth anniversary of the attacks, a hearse carrying Staff Sergeant Michael Ollis began making its way up Interstate 95.

The closer the white hearse got to Staten Island, the more American flags hung from overpasses and the more mourners began lining highways and streets to honor the fallen local soldier. "Welcome home, SSG Michael Ollis," one sign read. "We love you, Mike," said another. "Thank you for keeping us safe."

Mike's hearse was escorted up I-95 in a police motorcade that also included the Patriot Guard Riders and Rolling Thunder. On one of the lead motorcycles was Jimmy, who had been planning to throw a huge party for Mike's upcoming birthday when his friend came home from Afghanistan. Instead, Jimmy would wind up toasting Mike at his graveside with a six-pack of Bud Light.

Images from the motorcade, which included a dedicated traffic lane on the always busy Staten Island Expressway, were poignant and unforgettable. Fire trucks lined multiple overpasses flying huge American flags and also "9/11: Never Forget" signs. Police officers stood outside their NYPD vehicles and saluted. Several drivers in other lanes pulled over knowing only that something important was happening. Many construction workers stopped what they were doing, lowered their heads and put their hard hats over their hearts. Mourners of all ages waved their flags, shouted their support to the Ollis family, and shed their tears.

As they rode with their son's casket inside the limousine, Bob and Linda looked out the windows with astonishment. *Where did all these people come from? Is this really all for Michael?*

Indeed, it was all for him. Just as neighbors had greeted Bob and Linda with flowers and food when they first got back to their Burbank Avenue home from London and then Dover, thousands of neighbors they didn't know from across Staten Island and all of New York City had shown up to make sure they knew that their son's ultimate sacrifice was noticed and appreciated.

Bob and Linda happened to be looking out the window toward the same spot when they noticed an elderly man wearing his old US Marine Corps dress uniform near some train tracks. He was standing alone and saluting Mike as the hearse went by. The image instantly brought a tear to the grieving Gold Star father and combat veteran's eye.

"That's respect," Bob whispered to Linda while gently squeezing her hand.

Indeed, Staten Island was opening its arms for their son, just as Mike himself had promised to do for soldiers serving in the aftermath of 9/11, when he was only a teenager.

"Staten Island supports you and we will welcome you back when you come home," Mike once wrote in his high school journal.

There was complete silence at the funeral home as Mike's coffin was carried from the hearse and saluted by Tino, Jason, and every soldier and veteran who was standing outside under a large American flag being flown at half-staff in Mike's honor, as had officially been ordered by Mayor Bloomberg and Governor Cuomo. Jimmy, who was standing in front of the funeral home in his Rolling Thunder motorcycle vest, put his hand over his heart. Linda wept and so did Kim and Kelly, who was holding Mike's godson, Matthew.

Bob had both arms wrapped around his family while watching Mike's coffin being carried into the funeral home. Once the casket was inside, he would finally be allowed to reach out and touch it.

At the wake, hundreds of mourners waited in line for hours to pay their respects to their hometown hero. Those in attendance included prominent local politicians and even Cardinal Timothy Dolan, the Catholic Church's archbishop of New York. For the entirety of the viewing, Mike's casket was closely guarded by his fellow soldiers and friends.

On Burbank Avenue, the Ollis family home became a revolving door of supporters showing up with food, gifts, and donations to help with funeral expenses. That money would wind up helping create the Staff Sergeant Michael Ollis Freedom Foundation to help veterans, active duty troops, and military families.

At the end of Burbank Avenue, against a chain-link fence, Mike's friends and neighbors began leaving photos and other mementos that quickly turned into a makeshift memorial. Recognizing the site's significance, the NYPD soon put up barricades to make sure everyone knew that any mischief at the memorial would not be tolerated by police or anyone who lived in the neighborhood. As Jimmy put it, someone could have left a hundred-dollar bill on that fence and no one would have dared to touch it, let alone take it.

The night before the funeral, a candlelight vigil attended by approximately four hundred Staten Islanders was held at the nearby Great Kills Veterans Memorial. Bob and Linda watched in amazement as residents from all over their community continued to come out of the woodwork to honor their son.

Mike's funeral mass was held across the street from the funeral home at Our Lady Queen of Peace Roman Catholic Church on New Dorp Lane in Staten Island. Despite exhaustion, grief, and lingering questions about exactly how his son died, Bob nevertheless found the strength to stand up to speak. He talked about the heroism of his son and the wonderful family he left behind, including Kim, Bill, Kelly, Dave, and, most of all, his beloved nephews and niece: William, Joseph, Thomas, Matthew, and Ava.

Bob also pointed to three pews in the front of the beautiful church, all of which were packed with politicians who wanted to show support and pay their respects. After thanking them for being there, Bob asked the local, city, and state leaders to keep telling the stories of heroes like his only son, who was willing to lay down his life not only in the defense of his country but also for the people of Afghanistan and—as fate would have it—Poland.

Shortly after Bob sat down, took a deep breath, and collected himself, a family friend named Mike Powell stood up to read a letter at Bob and Linda's request. It was written by a soldier named TJ Petullo, who mailed the letter from FOB Ghazni just three days after Mike was killed:

> *Staff Sergeant Mike Ollis was the best squad leader I've had the privilege of working with during my brief time in*

the army. He enlisted right out of high school. We celebrated his 24th birthday last September out in California at the National Training Center and laughed about the Army's birthday plans for him over the years—basic training, Iraq, Afghanistan, field training in Louisiana, and back in Afghanistan again.

The first time I met him was during my second day at the battalion, running targetry during a live fire exercise. I still didn't know names by the end of the day—just knew him as the crazy team leader who ran around the whole exercise yelling at his men with his Staten Island accent. The only thing that matched his temper was his sense of humor—his crazy grin was pretty much a trademark for his platoon.

He went to Ranger School last April and came back with his Ranger tab in July (there aren't many sergeants in the Army that can say the same) and moved up to squad leader soon after. When there was a mundane job nobody else wanted to do—cleaning trucks, moving supplies—he wouldn't hesitate to volunteer and see it through. While every other leader was taking a break in a tent or in his office, Mike would still be out there with his guys doing the dirty work.

He was promoted to Staff Sergeant last year. He never got tired of messing with his new peers, his fellow squad leaders—the guys he used to work for as a team leader.

His dad, a combat infantry veteran of Vietnam, came up for a few days to visit in January before we deployed. He was identical—it was like catching a glimpse of Staff Sergeant Ollis in thirty years. Being around them, the pride they had in each other was palpable.

We came to Afghanistan in January and he contin-ued to be indispensable. He always knew how to fix vital equipment when everyone else could only stand around and scratch our heads. Not just for his platoon; for the company and sometimes the entire battalion. Day in and day out he commanded the lead truck on patrols or the lead element when on foot. He was utterly unfazed by tense situations, always level-headed and ready to roll. At the same time, he was a friendly goof with the local kids in the bazaars or at medical clinics.

Staff Sergeant Ollis re-enlisted back in February for six more years of service to our country. Here he was on his third deployment, probably working harder than just about anyone else, and volunteering for the better part of another decade.

He was the only squad leader in his platoon to be put in for a Bronze Star medal for his work on this deployment. Only two or three squad leaders out of over a dozen in the battalion received that honor. Earlier this month, he was selected to be a member of the Sergeant Audie Murphy Club, an incredibly prestigious group for outstanding non-commissioned officers in the Army. I've met hundreds of NCOs during my brief years in the Army, and only know four men (including Staff Sergeant Ollis) who are members.

Three days ago, he gave the final proof of the kind of man he was. While he was going to the computer café with seven of his soldiers, the FOB was attacked by a massive car bomb. Most people on the FOB reacted by moving to the nearest bunker for safety. Staff Sergeant Ollis made sure his guys were okay, got them to a bunker and took off toward a breach in the wall—with no armor, no helmet and just the one magazine of thirty rounds for his weapon.

[Staff Sergeant Ollis was] a man who was only passing through this FOB—we had only been here two days, and *he had a flight scheduled later that night to get up to Bagram Airfield. He was killed a few minutes later, preventing insurgents from getting further into the FOB through the breach. It's not an exaggeration to say that many other people would have died if Staff Sergeant Ollis and a few others hadn't run to the blast.*

He was the best of us, and we are lesser for his absence. I don't want condolences—pray for his family back home, and friends over here, who are no doubt hurting more than me. I'm writing this because I want you to know the kind of people who serve, and because a man like that deserves not to be forgotten as the years go by.

There wasn't a dry eye in the packed Catholic church at the end of TJ's moving letter or Bob's heartfelt speech. Slowly but surely, it was dawning on almost everyone—especially Bob, Linda, Kelly, and Kim—that what Mike had done that day at FOB Ghazni was both consequential and courageous.

As close friends and fellow soldiers served as Mike's pallbearers, all Tino could think about was the many military funerals that he and Mike had helped carry out while serving together at Fort Campbell. While every service member knows the danger of a combat deployment, Tino never imagined that he would one day be doing the same for Mike, who was always enthusiastic and serious about honoring fallen soldiers and veterans.

It was Tino and Jason who wound up presenting the folded American flag to Linda and Bob later that morning at the Cemetery of the Resurrection on the southern shore of Staten Island. As a light breeze gently cooled down the hundreds of mourners at the grave site, Brian Constantino—who had been so badly injured during his and Mike's second combat deployment together—uttered perhaps the most consequential words of his life.

"On behalf of the president of the United States, the United

States Army, and a grateful nation, please accept this flag as a symbol of our appreciation for your loved one's honorable and faithful service," Tino said while handing the folded flag to Linda.

"Thank you," Linda and Bob whispered in unison to their son's anguished fellow Iraq and Afghanistan veterans.

After a dramatic twenty-one-gun salute and a final Catholic prayer of committal at the conclusion of the burial service, tearful mourners began to slowly leave the Cemetery of the Resurrection. The following year, James Capodanno—the brother of one of Mike's childhood heroes, Medal of Honor recipient and Staten Island native Father Vincent Capodanno—would be buried only a few short yards away from Mike.

When the funeral was over, Mike's childhood friends went their separate ways while resolving to come back to their friend's graveside two days later for what would have been his twenty-fifth birthday. Little did Mike's best friends know that they would reunite much sooner—only a few minutes later, in fact.

"Let's go get some Mike burgers," Alanna said to Kristen as they got into a car together, even though they were both feeling nauseated after an excruciatingly emotional four days of funeral events.

As the clock struck noon, cars began arriving one by one at the White Castle fast-food restaurant on Hylan Boulevard in New Dorp. Alanna and Kristen showed up first, before Jimmy, Rob, Quaseem, and a few more childhood friends—including Bolivar, who had just been honorably discharged from the Marine Corps—all arrived in separate vehicles. No one had coordinated anything; the White Castle was simply the most fitting place to go for a close-knit group of friends who had known Mike since he was a short, skinny Staten Island boy who wanted to someday become a soldier like his dad.

For the next hour or so, Mike's childhood friends wiped away their tears and did what they know he would have wanted: share old stories that would make each other smile. Indeed, howls of laughter filled the small burger joint when Jimmy told the story of a tipsy Mike falling out of the back seat while reaching for his bag of cheeseburgers. Alanna told a similar story about Mike opening the door of her minivan over her protests one late night at the drive-thru.

"Here's to Mike," Rob said as everyone raised their soft drinks.

"To Mike!" his closest friends said together in unison.

For the rest of their lives—whether it was at birthdays, weddings, or even the births of their children—Mike would always be with Jimmy, Rob, Bolivar, Quaseem, Alanna, and Kristen. From boyhood to the day he died and well beyond, they were the best friends Mike ever could have asked for.

That night, everyone seemed to descend on the Ollis house for what would truly be a celebration of Mike's life. Scores of relatives, friends and Mike's army buddies—other than the still-deployed soldiers of Triple Deuce—filled Bob and Linda's Burbank Avenue home and legendary backyard. There was a palpable sense of sadness, but also camaraderie and laughter.

Two of the great women in Mike's life—Courtney and Katherine—were among the guests. As stories were told and the drinks began to flow, Courtney made a keen observation.

"This is what Michael lived for—getting his family and friends together," she said. "This is what he did all of this for. It was for us."

As Mike's nephews and niece grew up in the years following his death, Kim, Bill, Kelly, and Dave always made sure that Uncle Mike was a part of their children's many milestones and achievements:

> *Michael,*
> *I remember hearing your laugh. I remember all the great*
> *things you did with all the bravery and courage you had, too.*

Now we tell stories not like we used to. We tell stories about how much we miss you. I wish you were here so I could hear you laugh just one last time or feel the love of your hugs.

Though you may be gone now we love to talk about all the crazy things me and you would do. How we would play games in the hot summer or make snowmen in the freezing winter.

I love you and I wish you were here.

Ava Manzolillo

Mike's oldest nephew, William Loschiavo, wrote a college essay about Mike titled "Surprisingly Thankful":

"Deeds not words" has been a part of my life before I ever fully understood its meaning. To live your life in a way that can help others daily by your actions is how my parents are raising me. I have been blessed with many different experiences that have truly made me the person that I am, but one experience in particular has helped me strive to be the person I want to become.

The one experience that stands out in my life that I have felt made me surprisingly thankful for my freedom is the passing of my Uncle Michael in 2013. His actions have made me realize how thankful I am for the way I live my life. My Uncle Michael was killed in action in Ghazni, Afghanistan on August 28, 2013. The day we received the call has changed my life forever. From that day on, my life was never the same. I became a Gold Star family member. I learned how many other including my uncle sacrificed their lives so I can live my life the way I want to.

On the morning of August 28, I was woken up by my parents and they told me the news about his passing. I was lying in bed and my parents said, "Uncle Mike passed away." Hearing that news as a nine-year-old, I was confused and devastated. I broke down in tears in my father's arms and cried.

Ever since that morning, I have changed the way I view the world and that has made me surprisingly thankful for the things I have. One example of something I am surprisingly thankful for is my freedom. Before that day, I never really thought about my freedom as being a part of me. I never really understood or cared about the military and its purpose. I took my freedom for granted. I have always been able to voice my opinions at home and in school. I was surprised that many other children my age in this world do not have the freedom to choose what they want to do in life or what schools they want to attend as I have.

This reminds me of the time when my 5th grade class took a trip to Ellis Island in New York City to understand the history of immigration. This trip gave me a better understanding of the importance of immigration into our country and why their family members left their homelands in search of freedom and better opportunities. Both sides of my family, I learned that day, have roots planted in Ellis Island from Italy and Ireland. I was surprised to learn how difficult their lives were and how my great grandparents and great aunts and uncles struggled for freedom that had been dimmed by government control. If it wasn't for their brave sacrifices and leaving behind people they loved for a better future, I would not be able to partake in all of the freedoms our country of the United States of America has to offer. My light might have been dimmed.

The surprising death of my young uncle has really motivated me to get involved in my New Jersey community and my uncle's New York City community to volunteer.

In my hometown, I have volunteered weekly with the local VFW to help serve food to local veterans every week. I have also volunteered at the VFW Post #9587 in Staten Island, New York, where my uncle grew up. I have helped clean the VFW and organize their filing system and set up the local 5K races annually.

In conclusion, "deeds not words" will live within me for the rest of my life. It has taken on a new meaning in my life that gives me responsibility.

On November 12, 2013, Bob and Linda Ollis were presented with two more prestigious military awards that were posthumously bestowed on their son. To their initial surprise, the ceremony took place at the Polish consulate in New York City. It was on that day that Bob, Linda, Kelly, and Kim finally gained a full understanding of why so many people were telling them that Mike had died a hero:

The Polish Armed Forces Gold Medal is the only defense reward exclusively presented to foreign individuals as a token of appreciation for their outstanding performance and great devotion to support the Polish Armed Forces activities, including multinational overseas contingency operations.

Staff Sergeant Michael H. Ollis during an attack on a base in Ghazni shielded a Polish soldier, thereby saving his life. This act of valor affirms the brotherhood which links Polish and American soldiers in their fight against terrorism.

Poland's Minister of Defense Tomasz Siemoniak in recognition of his heroic and selfless actions in the line of duty has awarded SSG Michael H. Ollis the Polish Armed Forces Gold Medal.

Presented on this 12th day of November 2013 in the Consulate General of the Republic of Poland in New York.

The Afghanistan Star is the presidential reward exclusively presented to solders as a token of appreciation for their outstanding performance during the service in the Islamic Republic of Afghanistan.

SSG Michael H. Ollis' sacrifice in the line of duty is an ultimate manifestation of brotherhood in arms. His valor will never be forgotten. His courage will always be remembered.

The President of the Republic of Poland Bronisłw Komorowski in recognition of his selfless heroism and devotion has awarded SSG Michael H. Ollis the Afghanistan Star.

While some New York media outlets covered the event, the number of American journalists paled in comparison to the throng of Polish reporters who were itching to interview the parents of their country's newest hero.

"I did not realize that such a brotherhood exists between our two nations and soldiers," said Linda at the ceremony, as quoted by Radio Poland. "I'm impressed. I'm honored."

Numerous dignitaries also spoke at the ceremony.

"Poland and the United States have a long-standing relationship of friendship, cooperation and strategic alliance; it is this commitment that drove Sergeant Ollis and Lieutenant Cierpica to serve in Afghanistan," Polish Ambassador Ryszard Schnepf said.

"What [Mike] really represents to the world is humanity, for there is no greater gift than to give your life for someone else," added then congressman Michael Grimm, a Republican from New York.

While the Polish medals were incredibly significant, the November 2013 consulate ceremony marked the first time Bob and Linda had seen the soldiers of Triple Deuce since their son was killed. Due to the day's whirlwind of events, they didn't get to spend as much time as they wanted with the soldiers, who had come down for the event from Fort Drum. It had been almost three months since the attack on FOB Ghazni, but Mike's brothers-in-arms were still reeling from his death.

"I loved your son," a tearful Doyle said to Bob while shaking his hand and giving him a hug.

"I wanted to go with Mike, but Mike wouldn't let me," an emotional Eric said to Mike's parents. "He wanted me to stay back in the bunker. I'm so sorry."

Bob and Linda would get to talk more with the soldiers of Triple Deuce, including Schnell, Eddie, Patrick, Shane, and TJ, during a subsequent ceremony up at Fort Drum. While they still had questions, what immediately became clear to the entire Ollis family was that Mike would be a part of the Bushmaster 2–22nd Infantry Regiment, First Brigade Combat Team, Tenth Mountain Division brotherhood for life. If they ever needed anything, the soldiers of Triple Deuce would move mountains to help them.

There was another very special guest for Bob, Linda, Kim, and Kelly to meet at the consulate in Manhattan that day. In the lobby, they would have their first emotional encounter with the wounded Polish soldier who so adamantly credited Mike with saving his life: second lieutenant Karol Cierpica.

Karol, who, like his American counterparts at the ceremony, had just left the battlefield in Afghanistan—was visibly nervous and full of guilt. Would the fallen soldier's parents resent his presence at the ceremony since he was alive and their son was dead? Would the Ollis family be angry with him for not being able to save Mike's life after the suicide blast?

In that anxious moment, Bob opened his arms and gave the tormented Polish soldier a hug.

"Welcome to our family," he told Karol, who was stunned. "Welcome to our new friend. Thank you for your service."

"We love you," Linda added while joining the group hug, which soon included Kelly and Kim as well.

The still-grieving Ollis family's compassionate and genuine gesture would help Karol, who also leaned on his deep faith in God, battle depression and many years of survivor's guilt about the tragic events of August 28, 2013. It also symbolized unity between two families—and two countries—during a protracted and bloody war in Afghanistan that would last another eight excruciating years.

On January 11, 2015, a little boy was born in Kraków, Poland. His proud parents were Karol and Basia Cierpica.

Ten months later, the Cierpica family traveled to Staten Island for the unveiling of a new monument—a majestic eight-foot bronze statue of Mike carrying his M4 rifle and running toward the sounds of danger, much as he did on August 28, 2013. The Staff Sergeant Michael Ollis Freedom Plaza—located beneath an American flag next to the track he once ran around at the Michael J. Petrides School—also includes three stone monuments honoring fellow fallen military heroes from Staten Island.

"Mr. Robert and Mrs. Linda, I would like you to meet my wife, Basia, and my oldest son, Jacob," Karol said in his best possible English.

The Polish soldier then knelt beside a red stroller and held the hand of the ten-month-old baby boy, who was grasping a teddy bear.

"And this is Michael," Karol said.

After picking up the baby and his teddy bear, which was made for Michael out of Mike's old US Army fatigues by a nonprofit organization called the Matthew Freeman Project, Bob and Linda smiled at the baby as their eyes filled with tears.

"Hello, Little Michael!" Bob said. "You are our newest grandson."

Just as the family of US Army Staff Sergeant Michael Ollis had opened their arms for second lieutenant Karol Cierpica during their emotional first meeting, the Polish army officer had responded with a tribute that would resonate for decades to come.

"The presence of your son is always in our lives with the birth of my son," Karol said to Bob and Linda during a speech at the ceremony. "I will never let the memory of your son die."

After the Ollis family welcomed the Cierpicas into their home, they took a walk down their neighborhood street, where they could still picture little Mike running around playing war and staging ambushes on his neighbors. When they reached the now-permanent memorial that friends had started in the days after Mike's death, a shiny new green sign hung beneath an old one that said "Burbank Av."

"SSG Michael H. Ollis Way," the new sign read.

Even though he knew his ten-month-old son was too young to understand, Karol then pointed at the large picture of Mike that still stands in a wooden frame resting against the fence.

"That is your Uncle Michael," the Polish soldier said. "Your father is alive because of this very brave man, and so are you."

At some point during Michael Cierpica's life, the people of Poland and the United States will almost certainly be called upon to once again fight shoulder to shoulder against a common enemy. If and when that day arrives, the twenty-four brief but significant years that US Army Staff Sergeant Michael Ollis spent on earth can serve as a blueprint for any young man or woman who wishes to defend not only their nation, but the cause of freedom itself.

"My father thought it was a privilege to serve the country he lives in," Mike wrote as a young JROTC cadet. "And now, so do I."

EPILOGUE

LIVE LIKE MIKE

Bob and Linda Ollis still live on SSG Michael Ollis Way in the New Dorp neighborhood of Staten Island with their trusted service dog, Neville. The family's Staff Sergeant Michael Ollis Freedom Foundation continues to send care packages to deployed troops while also providing assistance to military families here at home. Additionally, the foundation runs service projects involving local schools and has established several scholarship programs to help students wanting to pursue careers as a US military service member, police officer, firefighter, or first responder.

Each June, the SSG Michael Ollis 5K Run and 2-Mile Walk is held in New Dorp. Since its 2016 inception, the Ollis 5K has grown into one of Staten Island's biggest annual running and walking events. Despite steady rain throughout the 2022 run, the event attracted approximately nine hundred runners and spectators, according to the *Staten Island Advance*.

Kim, Bill, Joseph, and Thomas Loschiavo still live in central New Jersey. Mike's oldest nephew, William Loschiavo, is currently a student at James Madison University in Harrisonburg, Virginia. Will's moving essay about Uncle Mike unquestionably helped him get accepted to JMU and several more schools.

Kelly, Dave, Ava, and Matthew Manzolillo once again live in Maryland after spending several years abroad in Germany. While living in Europe, they made multiple trips to Poland for events honoring Mike.

Courtney, Marissa, and Katherine are all married with children of their own. Even though Mike never got the chance to be a husband or father, he is most certainly smiling down on all the great women in his life as they raise families of their own.

Corporals Eddie Garcia and Patrick McTighe both became sergeants in the US Army. Both credited the example Mike set—as well as his incessant orders to study—for their eventual promotions.

"I spoke to Staff Sergeant Ollis and told him I did not want to go to the [promotions] board because I did not want to study and because I was nervous to be quizzed by the first sergeants. At the end of my conversation with Staff Sergeant Ollis, he told me he was not going to let me quit," Eddie wrote in a letter to Mike's parents. "Shortly after the board was over, I was given the news that I had passed. Once I came home, I received the rank of sergeant and that was only possible because of your son."

"Thank you for sponsoring me at the promotion board," Patrick wrote in an emotional letter to his fallen teammate. "It is so difficult to believe that you are not here with us."

As of 2023, Brian Schnell was still in the US Army as a first sergeant in command of about two hundred soldiers at Fort Drum. His office is in the same building where he and Mike used to work—and occasionally wrestle. Schnell's company is also located right next to Fort Drum's Staff Sergeant Michael H. Ollis Weapons Center, which was rededicated in 2019 with the fallen soldier's parents in attendance.

"Bob and Linda, thank you for teaching your son how to live a life of honor," US Army Lieutenant Colonel Rex Howry said on September 26, 2019. "Know that what I say here or what we do here cannot capture what your brave son gave in protection of others, but we can never forget what he did for our country."

"Sergeant Ollis made honor his mantra," the commander of Triple Deuce later added. "So, train like Mike; live like Mike. Deeds not words."

Every soldier and veteran whose name appears in this book has been welcomed with open arms by Bob, Linda, Kim, and Kelly. Just as Mike's father told Karol he was, who still lives in Poland with his wife and children—including young Michael—the brave warriors who once served by Mike's side are now members of the Ollis family.

Staff Sergeant Michael Ollis has received so many posthumous honors and awards that there are almost too many to list. None is more prominent than the Distinguished Service Cross—the second-highest award that can be bestowed on an American soldier. Mike's Silver Star was formally upgraded to the Distinguished Service Cross in 2019.

"Every generation has its heroes," said General James McConville, who traveled to Staten Island for the ceremony. "Michael Ollis is one of ours."

The ceremony was attended by state and local leaders as well as Mike's friends, fellow veterans, and members of the Ollis family—including Karol, who flew in from Poland.

"I was privileged to serve with Michael and Karol when I was the 101st Airborne Division commanding general in Regional Command East while they were deployed," General McConville said. "Their actions that day in August against a very determined enemy saved many, many lives."

"Karol is here today because of Michael's heroic actions on the 28th of August, 2013," the general said later in his remarks. "Karol, thank you from coming all the way from Poland."

Amid thunderous applause, General McConville saluted second lieutenant Cierpica, who returned the salute with tears in his eyes.

Bob also spoke at the packed event, which was held at a significant location: the Staff Sergeant Michael Ollis VFW Post 9587. The VFW, which Bob had been visiting for many years to socialize and organize events with his fellow veterans, was officially renamed after his son in 2014.

"It's painful to relive it. I've been approached by many people who say 'How the hell do you do it' and I don't know," Mike's proud father said at the Distinguished Service Cross ceremony. "But I think, like Karol, through the tears, we have to tell the story of Karol and Michael. They just locked arms and followed each other."

"They didn't worry about what language or what color it was," Bob continued. "It was two battle buddies . . . and that's what Karol and Michael did. To help everyone on that FOB that they possibly could."

The official US Army citation tells the selfless story of Mike's ultimate sacrifice:

> The President of the United States of America, authorized by act of Congress, 9 July 1918 (amended by act of 25 July 1963) has awarded the Distinguished Service Cross to Staff Sergeant Michael H. Ollis, United States Army.
>
> For extraordinary heroism while engaged in action against an enemy of the United States while serving as an infantryman with Company B, 2d Battalion, 22d Infantry Regiment on 28 August 2013 in Afghanistan. When a complex enemy attack involving vehicle-borne improvised explosive devices, suicide vests, indirect fire, and small arms fire against Forward Operating Base Ghazni began, Staff Sergeant Ollis ordered his fellow soldiers who were located in a building to move to bunkers to shield themselves from fire. After accounting for his soldiers, he re-entered the building to check for casualties and then

moved toward the enemy force which had penetrated the perimeter of the forward operating base.

Staff Sergeant Ollis located a coalition forces officer and together they moved toward the point of attack without their personal protection equipment and armed only with their rifles. Upon reaching the attack point, he and his comrade linked up with other friendly forces and began a coordinated effort to repulse the enemy from the airfield and adjacent buildings.

While under continuous small arms, indirect and rocket-propelled grenade fire, Staff Sergeant Ollis and his comrades moved from position to position engaging the enemy with accurate and effective fire. While fighting along the perimeter of the forward operating base, an insurgent came around a corner and immediately engaged them with small arms fire.

With complete disregard for his own safety, Staff Sergeant Ollis positioned himself between the insurgent and the coalition forces officer who has been wounded in both legs and was unable to walk. Staff Sergeant Ollis fired on the insurgent and incapacitated him, but as he approached the insurgent, the insurgent's suicide vest detonated, mortally wounding him.

Staff Sergeant Ollis' actions are in keeping with the highest traditions of the military service and reflect great credit upon himself, the 1st Brigade Combat Team, 10th Mountain Division, and the United States Army.

As of 2023, only twenty-two other soldiers had received the Distinguished Service Cross for heroism in combat since September 11, 2001, according to HomeOfHeroes.com, a military history website. While the award is rare and prestigious, some think

Mike deserves even higher recognition, including the majority leader of the United States Senate.

"Staff Sergeant Michael Ollis was among the best that our nation has to offer," Senator Schumer wrote in a letter to General McConville pushing for Mike's Distinguished Service Cross to be upgraded to the Medal of Honor. "He is the quintessence of what it means to be American, and his life is a testament to the values of the US Army and the United States of America."

As of 2023, Mike's Distinguished Service Cross, while deeply appreciated by the Ollis family, has yet to be upgraded.

So far, the only US service member to receive the Medal of Honor resulting from the FOB Ghazni attack is the soldier who held Mike in his last moments of consciousness before helping get him to the hospital: now US Army master sergeant Earl Plumlee. Earl received the nation's highest military award from President Joe Biden.

The nation's forty-sixth commander in chief spoke about the battle of Forward Operating Base Ghazni during the Medal of Honor ceremony, which was held at the White House on December 16, 2021:

> Outnumbered, with no regard for his own safety, at times armed with only a pistol, Staff Sergeant Plumlee attacked the insurgent forces, taking them on one by one. And time and again, bullets flew by, sometimes only inches away. And time and again, Staff Sergeant Plumlee closed with the enemy. And multiple occasions during the fight, the insurgents detonated their vests right in front of him—Plumlee—at one point hurling him into a wall and injuring his back.
>
> When a fellow soldier was severely wounded, Plumlee immediately ran to the soldier's position, carried him to safety, and administered tactical combat casualty care before returning to the fight.

When he learned that this book would be called *I Have Your Back,* the nation's newest Medal of Honor recipient reacted with enthusiasm, calling the title "perfect."

"I'm glad he had my back," Earl said of Mike.

Mike received many other US military awards in addition to the Distinguished Service Cross, Silver Star, two Bronze Stars, Purple Heart, and induction into the Sergeant Audie Murphy Club, which Bob and Linda accepted in their son's place. They include the Army Commendation Medal, Army Achievement Medal, Meritorious Unit Citation, Valorous Unit Award, two Army Good Conduct Medals, National Defense Medal, two Afghanistan Campaign Medals, Iraq Campaign Medal, Global War on Terrorism Service Medal, NCO Professional Development Ribbon, three Overseas Service Ribbons, NATO Medal, Ranger Tab, Combat Infantry Badge, Airborne Badge, Air Assault Badge, Drivers Wheel Badge, and Track Badge.

In 2021, Mike was inducted into the Tenth Mountain Division Warrior Legend Hall of Fame. The following year, an allied military regiment was renamed the Staff Sergeant Michael Ollis Junior Training Program.

"He showed me the true meaning of service, Michael did," said Karol during the allied naming ceremony, which was attended by Bob and Linda in Bydgoszcz, Poland, on March 18, 2022. "My true hero is an angel in heaven."

Many people in Poland revere US Army Staff Sergeant Michael Ollis, with memorial events and masses held annually in his honor. In July 2017, Polish president Andrzej Duda devoted a large section of a letter to then president Donald Trump to telling Mike's story.

"The additional, undoubted, strengthening element in our close relationship is the fraternity of arms among our soldiers, forged in Iraq, Afghanistan and other hotspots of the modern world. Especially, the action of a 24-year-old Staff Sergeant Michael H. Ollis, who during the Taliban attack on the base in Ghazni in August 2013, Afghanistan, gave his life shielding with his own body a Polish Lieutenant, Karol Cierpica, was firmly imprinted in the collective memory of the Polish people," President Duda wrote to his American counterpart. "For saving the life of a Polish officer, he was posthumously decorated by the Polish authorities with the Star of Afghanistan, and the Gold Medal of the Polish Army."

When President Trump addressed a large crowd in Warsaw during his subsequent trip to Poland, one of the portraits hanging from a building showed a familiar face: Staff Sergeant Michael Ollis. While Mike only got to visit the country once, his legacy endures in the hearts and minds of millions of grateful Polish citizens.

Of all the honors Mike and his family have rightfully received, the most unique was bestowed recently, and is a result of the tireless efforts of many New York leaders and supporters. In 2019, the first of three *Ollis*-class passenger ships to replace the aging Staten Island Ferry fleet was christened in Panama City, Florida. The ship's name would be the MV *SSG Michael H. Ollis.*

"I think it's really great that we're going to be christening a ship that is named after an American hero," said Florida governor Ron DeSantis at the November 27, 2019, ceremony held in Panama City. "When you look at Staff Sergeant Ollis—what he did, if you read the description—he basically put his life on the line to save other people. And had he not done that, he probably would have personally survived, but the people he was fighting with would have probably met their maker. So that is heroism."

The *Ollis*-class ships can each carry 4,500 passengers at a time and will wind up serving millions overall. While there were multiple delays building each ship due to hurricanes and the COVID-19 pandemic, the $85 million MV *SSG Michael H. Ollis* made its maiden voyage from Staten Island to Manhattan on Valentine's Day 2022.

Indeed, the launch ceremony, which was held at the St. George Ferry Terminal in Staten Island, was filled with love as Bob, Linda, and hundreds of family members and dignitaries braved cold weather to celebrate a massive ship being named for a hometown hero.

"[Former Staten Island borough president James] Oddo came over to me and said, 'Mr. and Mrs. Ollis, I don't want a boat named after me or another politician on this island, I want it named after your son,'" Bob said on February 14, 2022. "My jaw hit the ground."

The orange ship, which has Mike's name painted in huge white letters on its bow and life rings that say "SSG Michael H. Ollis," also has a gold-trimmed plaque on its main deck. For years to come, millions of passengers at the St. George and Whitehall terminals will be greeted by the story and smiling face of someone who not only rode the Staten Island Ferry countless times during his relatively short life but also gave everything he had to protect his city and country after both were attacked.

"When people get on this ferry for the first time—and they'll come from all over the world, like they always do—they'll ask 'Who's Michael Ollis?'" Staten Island borough president Vito Fossella said during the launch ceremony. "And they'll know he's the foundation of freedom."

For many who knew him, Staff Sergeant Michael Ollis's presence can be felt on the ship that is now named in his honor. That sensation might be strongest for Mike's childhood friend Bolivar Flores, who was once reassured by his fellow combat veteran as the Staten Island ferry they were riding sailed past the hallowed ground where the Twin Towers once stood.

"I understand what you're going through, man—I really do," Mike said to his friend, who was in anguish over his previous and upcoming Afghanistan deployments. "You can talk to me about this anytime."

On April 12, 2018, Bolivar welcomed a son. His name is Michael.

To this day, Bolivar and all of Mike's friends, fellow soldiers, and family members still talk to him, whether through prayer or in their own unique way. Somewhere, in a place that's undoubtedly less violent than the world he died defending, Mike is surely listening.

ACKNOWLEDGMENTS

On July 21, 2014—less than a year after Mike's death—I interviewed Bob and Linda Ollis by phone for a nationally syndicated column that was distributed to newspapers by Creators Syndicate.

"He was very, very proud of having two grandfathers who served and a father who served," Bob told me. "He always made me feel special [for serving] in Vietnam."

"We've received so many cards from people throughout the country, and gifts," Linda added. "Our neighbors have been unbelievable."

At the time, I was writing a column about a different American hero every week. While each story was special to my heart, something about Mike's stood out. Not only was I in awe of the young soldier's willingness to sacrifice his life to save a foreign service member he had only just met, but also by the way his story had quickly inspired so many, both in Poland and the United States.

In 2015, I wrote my first column for *The Stream* (stream .org)—where I am still a contributing senior editor—about Mike. In a subsequent interview for that article, Mike's parents told me about a trip they had just taken to Poland, where they were astonished by how their son's story had been embraced by the Polish people.

"A complete stranger walked up to us and said, in broken English, 'Are you the parents of the hero?'" Linda told me. "So many people knew who we were when we were there—they just honored Michael in so many different ways."

In 2017, I received a message from Mike's oldest sister, Kim Loschiavo, whom I had also made contact with while working on the two aforementioned articles. She told me that she lived in New Jersey and would be bringing her dad to one of my book-signing events, which was being held at my alma mater, Rutgers University in New Brunswick. Despite heavy rain, Kim and Bob made it to the event, which I deeply appreciated.

That night, Bob handed me a copy of the US Army investigative report about the FOB Ghazni attack and asked me to write a book about his son. Overwhelmed with gratitude by his request, I told Mike's dad and oldest sister that while getting any nonfiction book published can be a long and difficult journey, I would do everything I could to someday make it happen.

By March 2020, I had just about given up hope that this project would ever see the light of day. In fact, I sent an email apologizing to Bob and Linda for my failure to secure a publishing deal to share their son's story with the world. That all changed on January 21, 2022, when St. Martin's Press executive editor Marc Resnick—with whom I had worked on *Three Wise Men*—responded to a pitch email I had sent him with the words we had all been waiting for: "Let's make it happen!"

Marc, I am so grateful to you and the amazing St. Martin's Press team for the opportunity to work with all of you a second time. Without your expert guidance and steadfast belief in this book, Mike's story might never have been fully told.

To my agent, Greg Johnson, and his entire WordServe Literary Agency, thank you for also believing in Mike's story and playing an integral role in helping this project come to fruition.

To Mike's friends and fellow soldiers: this book would not be the same without your honest and heartfelt contributions. Thank you for taking the time to meet and/or speak with me by phone, as well as for answering my many text messages, emails, and follow-up calls with additional questions. Every day, you "live like Mike" and do your part to ensure that your friend and brother-in-arms is always remembered.

To Karol Cierpica: thank you for taking the time to speak with me from Poland over Zoom and to Marek Zalewski for translating our interview in real time.

To the Ollis family: What can I say except thank you? Throughout this process, you have welcomed me into your homes and communities as if I were a family member. I will never forget riding Mike's ferry ship with you, Bob and Linda, or taking another ferry trip a few months later with my wife and two daughters on our way to the Staten Island FerryHawks minor league baseball game being played in Mike's honor. Linda and Bob, the lovely gifts you gave our daughters, Reagan and Natalie, mean the world to Lisa and me. It's easy to see why every single person I've talked to has spoken so highly of your son: he has incredible parents.

Kelly and Dave: it was great to finally meet you, Ava, and Matthew at the game after you moved back from Germany. I look forward to spending more time with you in the years ahead.

Kim and Bill: thank you for inviting me to Will's awesome graduation party and for introducing me to him, Joey, and Thomas. After that party, I truly understood the bond shared by your family and friends. You are all such kind, welcoming, and patriotic people.

To my family: thank you for putting up with my stress while scrambling to meet yet another publishing deadline. If there winds up being a seventh book project, I promise to try to live less like Tom and more like Mike!

On a serious note, it has been the honor and privilege of a lifetime to research and write about the extraordinary life and legacy of US Army Staff Sergeant Michael Ollis. To paraphrase *Taking Chance,* the movie Linda thought of as her fallen son's flag-draped casket arrived at Dover, I didn't know Mike Ollis before he died. But today, I miss him.

ABOUT THE AUTHOR

Tom Sileo has authored or coauthored six military nonfiction books about heroes of America's post-9/11 wars in Afghanistan and Iraq. Those titles include *Three Wise Men,* his widely praised 2021 collaboration with combat veteran and Gold Star brother Beau Wise. Tom is a contributing senior editor for *The Stream* and a recipient of the Marine Corps Heritage Foundation's General Oliver P. Smith Award for distinguished reporting. He is a graduate of Rutgers University and lives in Delray Beach, Florida.